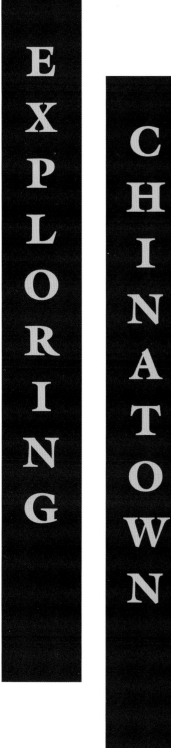

Exploring Chinatown

A Children's Guide to Chinese Culture

by Carol Stepanchuk

Illustrations by Leland Wong

Pacific View Press
Berkeley, California

To Bob, Sarah, Gregory, and John
— C.S.

*To my father, Suey Wing Wong, who encouraged me in my pursuit
as an artist. And my mother and wife for their patience.*
— L.W.

Acknowledgements

Special thanks to Pam Zumwalt for her editorial know-how and farsightedness and to Sue Gartley of Folk Art International for longtime support and assistance. To publisher Nancy Ippolito, editor Bob Schildgen, and designer Mark Ong, for producing books that make turning the pages worthwhile; to readers who gave generously of their time—Professor Alvin P. Cohen, University of Massachusetts, Amherst, and Professor Ellen Johnston Laing, University of Michigan; and helpful friends, David Lei, Dr. William Hu, Mark Ong, Kit Chow, Pi-Ping Savage, and Ying-Ying Lin Reed. To my husband, Bob, for suggestions that led to turning points; to my in-laws Blanche and Bill, relatives, and friends for their encouragement; to the memory of my parents and my aunt Marie, who set the foundation, and to Sarah and Gregory who continue the building.

The publisher would like to thank Robbin Henderson, Kit Chow, and Peter Mo Woo for their generous assistance in various aspects of the production. Also Chinatown Restaurant, 744 Washington Street, San Francisco for the use of their menu and to the students and directors of Leung's White Crane Martial Arts School, 32 St. Louis Place, San Francisco.

Credits:

Leland Wong, illustrations: cover, pages 4, 5, 6, 14, 16, 18, 19, 24, 30, 32, 33, 36, 42, 46, 52, 57, 58, 59

Angel Island poetry from *Island* by Him Mark Lai, et al., reprinted by permission of University of Washington Press: page 19

Lattice designs from *Chinese Lattice Designs* by Daniel Sheets Dye, reprinted by permission of Dover Publications: page 27

Peter Mo Woo, Chinese calligraphy: pages 20, 22, 23 and painting on page 49

Photo credits:

"Summer Mountains, Misty Rain," 1668, by Wang Hui, Asian Art Museum of San Francisco, The Avery Brundage Collection, Chong-Moon Lee Center for Asian Art and Culture: page 48

Cypress Book Company, San Francisco and Foreign Languages Press, Beijing: page 37

Smith Novelty, San Francisco: page 45

"Waiting for the Car," by Arnold Genthe (1868–1942), California Historical Society; FN-24891: page 41

Chinese Information and Culture Center, Taipei Economic and Cultural Office, New York: pages 21 and 55

"Taoist Priest's Robe," Minneapolis Institute of Arts, The John R. Van Derlip Fund: page 44

Ron Scherl, 2002, page 54

Karen Scroggs, pages 10, 11, 28

Carol Stepanchuk, page 44

Nancy Ippolito, pages 15, 34, 35, 56

Text copyright © 2002 by Carol Stepanchuk
Illustrations copyright © 2002 by Leland Wong
Cover and text design by Mark Ong

Library of Congress Catalog Card Number: LC 2001036661
ISBN 1-881896-25-0
Printed in China by Twin Age Limited.

Library of Congress Cataloging-in-Publication Data
Stepanchuk, Carol.
    Exploring Chinese culture : a children's guide to China-
        town / by Carol Stepanchuk ;
    Illustrations by Leland Wong.
        p.cm.
        Includes bibliographical references and index.
    ISBN 1-881896-25-0
    1. Chinese Americans—Social life and customs—Juvenile
        literature. 2. China—Social life and customs—Juvenile
        literature. I. Wong, Leland, ill. II. Title.
E184.C5 S82 2001
305.8951073—dc21   2001036661

CONTENTS

It's late morning and Chinatown is busy. Local people on errands and camera-clutching tourists share narrow sidewalks with displays of vegetables, fresh fish, and newspapers. Double-parked trucks unload meat, fruit, and more vegetables. Women workers from a garment factory take a short break in the sunshine. A column of preschoolers and their teachers head for the park, where groups of elderly men are settled into their games of Chinese chess. People are speaking Cantonese, English, Mandarin, Toishanese, and also Vietnamese.

Later, as afternoon shadows lengthen, backpack-laden children head for home or after-school Chinese school. Tourists still browse the souvenir shops. Packed city buses return workers from jobs throughout the city. Restaurant employees prepare for the evening rush. Colorful neon shop signs flick on. Cooking aromas fill the air. Grocers haul in their displays, wash down the sidewalk, and haul out the trash. Eventually the last diner and tourist leave, the last shop window is shuttered, the last restaurant worker closes up and goes home. The night's fog finally brings quiet.

Neighborhood. Tourist destination. Home. Workplace. Haven for the newly arrived, a place where the well-established can touch their roots. Welcome to Chinatown!

Our story begins in the 1850s, during the California Gold Rush. In San Francisco, Sacramento, and other towns Chinese merchants opened laundries, grocery shops, and restaurants to serve the Chinese and others who had come to California to mine for gold. When the gold boom ended, some Chinese returned home to China, but many found other jobs—construction, railroad building, farm work, and fishing—throughout the West. In the 1870s an economic recession spawned a wave of anti-Chinese violence. Newspapers, big business, politicians, and even labor leaders crusaded against the Chinese. The Chinese lost jobs, were attacked by mobs, and saw their businesses destroyed. Some went East. Many found a haven in San Francisco. Excluded from the mainstream, the Chinese responded to distrust and prejudice by creating their own community and economy. Chinatown, with its shops, businesses, and meeting places, grew up next to the city's business district. Today times and laws have changed, but America's Chinatowns continue.

Everyone, it seems, visits Chinatown. Chinese Americans come to see family and friends and to honor their traditions. They are proud of their language, accomplishments, history, foods, and customs. Other visitors come to learn about and experience Chinese culture. Chinatown isn't China, but its restaurants, markets, stores, herbal shops, temples, and art galleries offer everyone a lively peek at ideas and skills developed over centuries.

This book takes you on a cultural tour of Chinatown. You'll learn about seals and scrolls, mooncakes and moon guitars, lion dancing and laisee. You'll learn about names, numbers, families, and gods. You'll also learn more about how Chinatowns came to be. Our journey is based on San Francisco's Chinatown. Your city may have its own "Chinatown"— a unique neighborhood that shares this story and blends Asian and American cultures.

Come and visit!

SOJOURNERS

In the 19th century, most Chinese who headed to California were young men, sojourners from the Guangzhou (Canton) region, who expected to go back to China in a few years. Some had wives who stayed behind with the husband's family, tending children and helping maintain the household. If a man found work, he sent money home regularly. With luck and hard work, he might return to China a wealthy man. Some decided to settle and sent for wives and family. Still, travel was expensive, and many couldn't afford to have their families come. By 1870, of 48,000 Chinese in California, only about 3,500 were women.

In Hawaii the situation was different. Beginning in 1850, Chinese, both men and women, were recruited to work on American-owned sugar plantations. Men were encouraged to bring their wives and families. Chinese women continued to emigrate to Hawaii until 1898, when it was annexed by the United States and became subject to U.S. immigration laws.

吃過了沒有

Chiguole meiyou?
Have you eaten yet?

—*a traditional greeting
between friends, like "hello!"*

Whole roasted ducks hanging in store windows. The smell of pan-fried noodles. Fruits and vegetables in sidewalk displays. Live fish in tanks. Meat markets, delis, bakeries, restaurants, teahouses. Delivery trucks waiting to unload. Food everywhere you look. Restaurants, cafes, and prepared-food shops form the biggest piece of Chinatown's economy. Next come grocery stores and meat and fish markets.

Since Chinatown's earliest days, many people have made their living from rice, bamboo shoots, and soy sauce. Today most shops and restaurants are still family-owned. The food business does more than supply necessities and regional foods; it's a main source of jobs for newcomers.

Eating Out

A restaurant is where many people first begin to learn about Chinese culture. They try out chopsticks and sample the flavors and foods of China. They look at Chinese writing and hear Chinese spoken—Cantonese, Mandarin, or perhaps Toishanese. The restaurant may be large, with highly trained chefs, an extensive menu of elaborate dishes, and a banquet room for weddings and parties. Beautiful carvings, traditional paintings, and elegant furniture may grace the room. Or it may be a simple family restaurant serving quick, tasty standards, with waiters and family members peeling garlic and folding napkins at a back table during quiet moments.

A formal Chinese meal consists of many dishes, to be shared by all. In restaurants, big round tables allow everyone to reach the serving dishes. The host (or the parent) orders carefully, striving for a balance of tastes, textures, and aromas. This means contrasting sweet with sour, hot with cold, plain with spicy.

A well-selected meal includes dishes from the menu's various categories—seafood, poultry, pork, beef, vegetables. How many dishes? For a banquet, one per diner plus soup and rice!

Of course, not every meal is a formal, nine-course affair. At lunchtime, many diners choose quick, one-dish meals. Plates of rice, served with meat and vegetable toppings, are popular. Noodle shops and small cafes serve inexpensive soups and dumplings. Carry-out shops offer roasted meats and hot dishes, bakeries sell meat-and-vegetable-stuffed buns and pastries.

頭 樓 APPETIZERS

1. 鍋 貼	Pot Stickers (6)	4.55
2. 春 卷	Vegetable Spring Rolls (4)	4.25
3. 蔥 油 餅	Onion Cake	4.25
4. 炸 雲 吞	Fried Won Tons with Special Sauce	3.85
5. 辣 白 菜	Chinatown Special Cabbage	4.25
6. 棒 棒 雞 ♪	Ban Ban Chicken	4.25
7. 涼 拌 雞 絲	Chicken Salad	4.25
8. 海 鮮 沙 律	Seafood Salad	4.95
9. 燻 魚	Smoked Fish	5.25
10. 富 貴 雞 ♪	Chicken Wings	5.25
11. 五 香 牛 肉	Five Spice Beef	4.95
12. 麻 辣 肚 絲 ♪	Hot & Spicy Beef Tripe	4.95
13. 花 生 小 魚	Small Fish with Peanuts	5.50
14. 鹽 水 花 生	Peanuts with Five Spices	4.25
15. 小 籠 飽	Steamed Pork Dumplings (6)	4.55
16. 水 餃	Dumplings	4.55
17. 素 菜 飽	Steamed Vegetable Dumplings (4)	5.25

湯 類 SOUP

		S	L
18. 酸 辣 湯 ♪	Hot & Sour Soup	4.25	6.25
19. 西湖牛肉羹	West Lake Minced Beef Soup	4.25	6.25
20. 雞茸玉米湯	Chicken Corn Soup	4.25	6.25
21. 雲 吞 湯	Wonton Soup	4.25	6.25
22. 海鮮豆腐湯	Seafood and Bean Curd Soup	4.75	6.50
23. 鍋 巴 湯	Sizzling Rice Soup	5.00	7.25
24. 菠 菜 湯	Spinach and Bean Curd Soup	4.00	6.25
25. 魚 生 湯	Fresh Fish Soup	5.00	10.00

豬 肉 類 PORK

26. 香 乾 肉 絲 ♪	Pork with Dried Bean Curd	7.75
27. 京 醬 肉 絲	Bean Sauce Pork	7.50
28. 咕 嚕 肉	Sweet and Sour Pork	7.50
29. 糖醋排骨	Sweet and Sour Ribs (Shanghai Style)	7.50
30. 木 須 肉	Mu Shu Pork (4 Pan Cakes)	7.50
31. 回 鍋 肉 ♪	Twice Cooked Pork	7.50
32. 麻 婆 豆 腐 ♪	Ma Po Bean Curd	6.75
33. 湖南燻肉 ♪	Hunan Smoked Pork	7.95
34. 榨菜燒肉絲	Pork with Preserved Mustard Greens	7.50
35. 魚 香 肉 絲 ♪	Fish Flavored Pork	7.50
36. 上 海 豬 排	Shanghai Style Pork Chops	7.95

♪ Hot & Spicy

雞 鴨 類 POULTRY

37. 宮 保 雞 ♪	Kung Pao Chicken	7.75
38. 腰 果 雞	Cashew Nut Chicken	7.75
39. 芒 菜 雞 ♪	Mango Chicken	7.75
40. 醬 爆 雞	Bean Sauce Chicken	7.75
41. 辣 子 雞 ♪	Hot Pepper Chicken	7.75
42. 左宗棠雞 ♪	General Tsou's Chicken	7.75
43. 咖 哩 雞 ♪	Curry Chicken	7.75
44. 蘑 菇 雞 片	Moo Goo Gai Pan	7.75
45. 生 炒 雞 片	Shanghai Velvet Chicken	7.75
46. 檸 檬 雞	Lemon Sauce Chicken	7.75
47. 東 安 雞 ♪	Tung An Chicken	7.75
48. 香 酥 雞	Crispy Chicken (Half)	8.50
49. 樟 茶 鴨	Smoked Tea Duck (Half)	10.75
50. 香 酥 鴨	Crispy Duck (Half)	10.75
51. 北 京 鴨	Peking Duck	23.50
52. 雞 鬆	Chicken Lettuce Blossom	8.75
53. 甜 酸 雞	Sweet & Sour Chicken	7.75

牛肉、羊肉 BEEF AND LAMB

54. 四 川 牛 肉 ♪	Szechuan Beef	8.25
55. 蒙 古 牛 肉 ♪	Mongolian Beef	8.25
56. 沙 茶 牛 肉 ♪	Bar - B - Q Beef	8.25
57. 蔥 爆 牛 肉	Green Onion Beef	8.25
58. 青 菜 牛 肉	Beef with Tender Greens	8.25
59. 蠔 油 牛 肉	Oyster Sauce Beef	8.25
60. 西 蘭 牛 肉	Broccoli Beef	8.25
61. 蘭 豆 牛 肉	Beef with Snow Peas	8.25
62. 青 椒 牛 肉	Green Pepper Beef	8.25
63. 西 芹 牛 肉	Celery Beef	8.25
64. 乾 煸 牛 肉 絲 ♪	Dry - Sauteed Beef	8.25
65. 蔥 爆 羊 肉	Green Onion Lamb	9.95
66. 四季豆牛肉 ♪	Beef with String Beans	8.25
67. 中國城火鍋牛肉蝦	Chinatown Hot Pot w/ Beef & Prawns	13.95

海 鮮 類 SEAFOOD

68. 鴛 鴦 蝦	Special Twin Prawns	11.95
69. 四 川 乾 貝 ♪	Szechuan Scallops	11.95
70. 酸 菜 魷 魚	Squid with Pickled Cabbage	8.95
71. 清 炒 蝦 ♪	Shrimp a la Shanghai	10.75
72. 宮 保 蝦 ♪	Kung Pao Prawns	10.75
73. 核 桃 蝦	Walnut Prawns	10.75
74. 脆 炸 魚 ♪	Shanghai Crispy Fried Fish	10.75
75. 炒 三 鮮	Three Ingredients Seafood	12.95
76. 糖 醋 魚	Sweet and Sour Fish	Seasonal
77. 乾 燒 魚 ♪	Hot Braised Fish	Seasonal
78. 海 鮮 大 燴	Seafood Special	16.50
79. 乾 燒 明 蝦 ♪	Braised Prawns (with Shell)	11.95

特別介紹 Chef's Recommendations

C1. 豉 汁 大 蜆	Clams in Black Bean Sauce	9.95
C2. 清 蒸 魚 ♪	Steamed Fish	Seasonal
C3. 薑 蔥 蟹	Crab Sauteed w/ Ginger and Green Onions	Seasonal
C4. 椒 鹽 蟹	Salt and Pepper Crab	Seasonal
C5. 各 式 龍 蝦	Lobster Delight	Seasonal
C6. 上海式炒蝦仁	Shanghai Style Shrimp	16.95
C7. 椒 鹽 鮮 魷 ♪	Salt and Pepper Squid	12.50
C8. 玉 米 雞 球	Chicken Corn and Chinese Herb	12.50

蔬 菜 類 VEGETABLES

80. 麻 婆 豆 腐 ♪	Ma Po Bean Curd (No Meat)	6.25
81. 冬 菇 菜 心	Black Mushroom with Tender Greens	6.25
82. 開 洋 白 菜	Dry Shrimp with Chinese Cabbage	6.25
83. 壹 什 錦	Mixed Vegetable Deluxe	6.25
84. 乾 煸 四 季 豆 ♪	Dry Braised Green Beans	6.95
85. 魚 香 茄 子 ♪	Fish Flavored Eggplant	6.95
86. 素 炒 三 鮮	Three Ingredients Vegetables	6.25
87. 清 炒 菜 遠	Sauteed Seasonal Vegetables	6.25
88. 蠔 油 芥 蘭	Chinese Broccoli with Oyster Sauce	6.95
89. 紅 燒 豆 腐	Braised Bean Curd	6.25
90. 家 常 豆 腐 ♪	Family Style Bean Curd	6.25
91. 土 豆 絲 ♪	Sauteed Shredded Potato	6.25
92. 時 菜	House Special Vegetable	6.95

飯 麵 類 RICE AND NOODLES

93. 揚 州 炒 飯	Yang Chow Fried Rice	7.50
94. 四 川 炒 飯 ♪	Chef's Fried Rice	7.50
95. 蝦 炒 飯	Shrimp Fried Rice	6.75
96. 牛 炒 飯	Beef Fried Rice	6.75
97. 雞 絲 炒 飯	Chicken Fried Rice	6.75
98. 肉 炒 飯	Pork Fried Rice	6.75
99. 什 錦 炒 麵	House Special Chow Mein	7.50
100. 雞 絲 炒 麵	Chicken Chow Mein	7.50
101. 蝦 炒 麵	Shrimp Chow Mein	7.50
102. 沙茶牛肉炒麵 ♪	B.B.Q. Beef Chow Mein	7.50
103. 肉 絲 炒 麵	Pork Chow Mein	7.50
104. 白 飯	Steamed Rice	1.00

甜 品 類 DESSERTS

105. 芝 麻 湯 圓	Sesame Rice Ball Soup	3.50
106. 紅 豆 圓 仔	Red Bean / Rice Ball Soup	3.50
107. 名 牌 咖 啡	House Special Coffee	2.25
108. 香 濃 咖 啡	House Special Expresso	2.25
109. 冰 淇 淋	Assorted Ice Cream	2.25

♪ Hot & Spicy

A bilingual menu, organized by category

Yang foods include eggs, beef, and ginger. Yin foods include most vegetables, most fruits, *doufu,* bean sprouts, and many types of fish and seafood (but not shrimp). Sometimes foods change from yin to yang, or vice versa, depending on how they are cooked.

Style—You Are What You Eat

Although China has many distinct regional cuisines, it's the tastes of China's far south that most people know. Chinatown restaurants have served Cantonese food since the first laborers arrived from Guangdong's jagged coast in the 1850s. They brought with them the flavors and traditions of their tropical river valleys and delta lands. Here, lush greens and tropical fruits grow year-round. Paddy fields produce two or three crops of rice a year. Ponds, canals, and the sea provide fresh fish and shellfish as well as water-loving edible shoots, tubers, roots, and sprouts. Cantonese cooks stir-fry or steam this bounty lightly, so it won't lose fresh flavors and textures.

Chinese food first became popular with non-Chinese during the Gold Rush. Gold miners, tired of the beans and bread of the mining camps, discovered that they could get a good meal in the small restaurants run by enterprising Chinese. The popularity of Cantonese food brought a steady stream of diners into Chinatowns long after the Gold Rush ended. Restaurants continued to create job and business opportunities for Chinese Americans in many towns and cities. In the late 1960s, Americans began to discover other styles of Chinese food. New immigrants from other regions of China brought the spicy flavors of Sichuan and Hunan, the wheat noodles and dumplings of the North, and the stewed meats of Shanghai. Today it's possible to eat food from almost every part of China's vast countryside.

Home Cooking

Home-style Chinese cooking also pays attention to rules of balance. In China, the daily diet was, and still is based on *fan,* grains (rice, in the south, or wheat or millet, in the north) accompanied by *cai* (vegetables) and a little *doufu* (tofu, soybean curd), chicken, eggs, pork, or fish. Traditional ideas on health emphasize balancing the body's energy by eating the right foods at the right time. Eating the right foods for the season is important, too. Some foods are *yang* (hot), others are *yin* (cold), and a few are neutral. If you are feeling sluggish, and don't have enough energy you should eat more warm yang foods to "raise the heat." If you've gotten a rash, maybe you've eaten too many rich yang foods, and need to eat cool yin foods to "put out the fire."

Fried Rice

Here's a Cantonese, home-style recipe that uses leftover rice.

2 tablespoons vegetable oil

½ onion, minced

1 tablespoon fresh ginger, peeled, minced

1 cup Chinese barbecued pork or cooked ham, diced, or small cooked shrimps (or a combination)

4 cups cold, cooked rice

1 tablespoon soy sauce (add to the eggs)

2 eggs, beaten

½ cup peas, frozen or fresh

2 scallions (green onions), minced

pepper

(sesame oil—optional)

To stir-fry means to constantly stir and gently toss with a spatula while frying. If you don't have a wok, use a heavy skillet.

Chop and measure ingredients, beat eggs, and add soy sauce to eggs.

Heat wok or large skillet. When hot, add oil, then onion and ginger. Stir-fry 10 seconds, then add meat or shrimp. Continue to stir-fry over high heat for 2 minutes.

Add rice and cook over high heat (stirring as necessary) for another 2 minutes. Pour eggs over rice, mix well, and cook another minute.

Add peas and continue to stir-fry about 30 seconds. Taste. Add more soy sauce if you want. Spoon onto a platter. Top with scallions. Sprinkle with sesame oil and white pepper. Serves 4.

FOOD FACTS
- Chinese cooks developed stir-frying, *chao,* centuries ago. They realized that meat and vegetables cut into small pieces would cook fast.
- The wide, curved wok which cooks evenly and quickly was in use by the Tang dynasty (618–907). Its shape concentrates the heat and saves on fuel, something always scarce in China.
- The technique of steaming food, which also saves fuel, is even older. Archaeologists have found bronze steamers from the Shang dynasty (1600–1027 B.C.E.) that enabled cooks to prepare several dishes at the same time over the same fire.
- Chopsticks were in use 3,000 years ago.

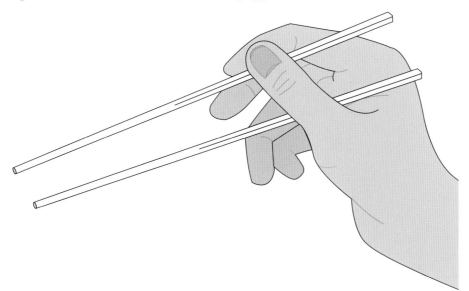

Tea

At every restaurant, a pot of tea arrives with the menus. Grocery stores sell dozens of kinds of tea in colorful cans and boxes. Tea shops may offer over 50 varieties, some for everyday drinking, some, very expensive, for connoisseurs.

Tea is as deeply intertwined with Chinese history as its art or literature. Tea was enjoyed throughout China by the seventh or eighth century. It's a beverage, a health enhancer, and a social custom. People have gathered to socialize in teahouses since at least the Song dynasty (960–1279). Poets wrote in them and about them. Artists painted them. Tea is still China's most valuable agricultural crop. All tea is made from the leaves of the same plant, *camellia sinensis,* a relative of the familiar flowering camellia. Differences in climate, soil, and processing influence the flavor. Green tea is made by drying the hand-picked leaves with heat. Black tea, called red tea in China, is made by crushing the leaves a little to bruise them, then allowing them to "ferment" (actually, oxidize) before drying. Oolong tea is also fermented, but for less time. Here are a few readily available kinds:

Lung Ching *(Longjing),* **Dragon Well:** a famous green tea, it makes a beautiful beverage with a mellow flavor. Green teas are especially popular in hot weather.

Gunpowder *(Pingshuizhu):* a strong-flavored green tea. During the drying process, the leaves are rolled into tiny pellets. They unfold in hot water. This tea contains fluoride, and in China is considered good for teeth.

Pu-erh *(Pu'er):* an earthy oolong; it soothes indigestion.

Tieh Kwan Yin *(Tie Guanyin):* a mellow oolong, named after the Buddhist Goddess of Mercy.

Keemun *(Qihong):* a high-quality black tea. Black teas are most popular in South China.

Jasmine *(Moli hua):* green tea dried together with fragrant jasmine flowers, a favorite in Beijing.

Lichee *(Lichi):* black tea treated with juice from lichi fruit, which adds a delicious, fruity flavor.

The Teahouse

In Chinatown, people gather for tea in cafes, bakeries, restaurants, and teahouses. Some teahouses offer tea in the *gongfu* style. Tea, usually *oolong*, is brewed in a very small teapot made of special clay that is said to hold the tea's flavor. Hot water is poured over the tea leaves to get rid of the bitterness, then, after a minute, poured off and discarded. More hot water is poured on the tea leaves. This batch is to drink. It is fragrant, somewhat like freshly cut grass. The tea is poured into tiny cups, to be sipped and savored.

Dimsum (Dianxin)

In the mornings, some teahouses are jammed with people who have come to *yincha (yumcha)* "drink tea" and eat dimsum. Servers patrol the room, pushing carts loaded with stacks of small bamboo or metal steamers. A diner calls one over. Uncovering a steamer, the server reveals bite-size sweet and savory treats. Maybe crescent dumplings stuffed with pork and black mushrooms. Maybe fat shrimp in a translucent wrapper. Maybe spareribs in black bean sauce. Another cart holds plates of round, sesame-covered balls with sweet lotus filling, and banana-leaf-wrapped bundles of sticky rice and chicken. The carts keep coming. A big restaurant may serve over 100 kinds of dimsum. In most places there's no menu. You choose what you want from the carts and the server stamps your card to keep track. It's hard to resist picking more than you can eat!

It's an old custom. In China, teahouses that served snacks with tea were popular by the tenth century.

A tiny parrot finch with feathers the color of the rainbow sings from an antique bamboo cage. A man sitting at a nearby table whistles a song in return. Another, ready to leave, places his birdcage in a shopping bag. "*Zaijian,* good-by." At this teahouse people gather to show off their songbirds. In old China this custom was popular with scholars and gentlemen. Today in China the bird owners are more likely to be retired workers and bird fanciers, who gather in parks. New immigrants to Chinatown often bring along traditional customs and ways, helping to keep Chinatown culture alive and tied to its roots.

The Market

Shoppers wind their way through Stockton Street markets, past cardboard boxes brimming over with dried shrimp, ginger tubers, fresh, knobby water chestnuts, and taro. Hand-written signs in Chinese characters tell what is for sale. Net bags hold big durian, (a large spiky, smelly fruit from Southeast Asia), and small lichi-like rambutan from Vietnam. Preserved eggs fill large brown pottery crocks. Shoppers pick carefully through eggplants, long beans, bitter melon, and several kinds of Chinese cabbage, seeking the freshest. Shop owners carry away empty boxes and bring out full ones. Customers debate prices in Cantonese, Toishanese, and Mandarin.

Today Chinatown grocery stores have freezer sections stocked with packaged dumplings and tropical juices. Refrigerator cases hold soy milk, eggs, and fresh noodles. But most of what's in the store reflects time-honored pre-refrigeration ways of preserving bountiful harvests. There are jars and cans of pickled vegetables, to eat with rice, or to use in soups and stir-fry. Dried foods include many types of fish, thin sheets or rope-like lengths of soybean curd, mushrooms, fruits, vegetables, and beans. There is a big selection of dried noodles—clear ones made from beans, rice flour noodles of various widths, and wheat noodles. Look for bags of wood ears (a wrinkly dry fungus), round black (shitake) mushrooms, and *facai* (black moss) which looks like black hair. It's added to New Year soups because its name means "money and wealth"—a good wish for the coming year.

Near bottles of soy sauce and sesame oil (used for flavor and fragrance) you'll find jars of fermented bean curd, called *furu,* and bright red chili oil. Red chili peppers, peppery preserves, and tangy spices are popular in southern and central China.

Holiday Treats and Everyday Snacks

In winter, shoppers crowd Chinese groceries to buy New Year foods. Along with oranges, tangerines, and *niangau (niangow)* "sticky rice cakes," they'll look for candied fruits and nuts for their New Year Tray of Togetherness. They'll select six or eight varieties of these treats. Each item stands for a particular type of good fortune. Strips of sugared coconut (a favorite with children) symbolize togetherness. Candied kumquats mean money because the Chinese character for "kum" also means "gold." Sugary lotus seeds send a wish for "many children."

In the fall, before the Moon Festival, bright red and gold mooncake cans are stacked everywhere in groceries and bakeries. Shoppers ponder the many assortments in the square tins, or stand in line at bakeries to select their own. Mooncakes are pastries with sweet, dense fillings. They are formed in molds with special designs. The most popular fillings are red bean paste, lotus paste, and nuts and seeds. Some have a whole cooked duck egg yolk inside to represent the moon.

For everyday snacking, Chinatown groceries carry dried fruits—sweet or salty plums, red prunes, hot and sour mango, yellow olives, star fruit—lobster crackers, dried fish, dried seaweed, meat jerky, and shrimp chips. Children usually prefer the coconut "puddings," haw flakes, juice boxes in tropical flavors, and cookies!

Mealtime Manners

"Don't make rice balls at the table; don't put fish you have been eating back on the serving plate; and don't pick your teeth at the table." —*Dining rules for Chinese scholars from the fourth century* B.C.E.

- At banquets always try to politely serve the person next to you before helping yourself.
- Select pieces closest to you—don't pick and choose.
- Wait until your parents, elders, or guests have started eating before you do.
- Don't overeat—the perfect number of servings will make you only *qifen bao,* "70% full," but make sure you don't leave a single grain of rice on your plate. That's wasteful. But, at banquets, be sure to leave a little food on your plate to show you are not greedy.
- When you're taking a rest from eating, place the chopsticks across the top of the rice bowl. Never stick the chopsticks straight up and down into the rice. That resembles incense sticks placed in an urn of sand on altars and at funerals.
- It's okay to hold your rice bowl close to your mouth with one hand while eating rice with chopsticks.
- Don't pile up your plate: take small servings. Food is usually served in courses, and more is coming!
- It's not polite to pour soy sauce on everything.

The early immigrants preferred food and flavors from home. Ships loaded with tea, rice, ginger tubers, soy sauce, and preserved foods sailed regularly from China to supply Chinatown markets. During the 1860s and 1870s, thousands of Chinese railroad-builders stayed healthy and strong on meals of dried oysters, cuttlefish, fruit and vegetables, noodles, rice, and soybean curd. Today stores are stocked with hundreds of food products from China, Taiwan, and Hong Kong, as well as the United States.

Shoppers can also find foods from Thailand, Vietnam, and Cambodia, the birthplaces of many ethnic Chinese immigrants. Groceries stock coconut milk, green mangoes, curry pastes, lemon grass, tropical fruits, French baguettes, and Vietnamese-style mooncakes and New Year treats.

飯後三百步，不用開藥鋪
Fanhou sanbaibu, buyong kai yaopu.
After meals, walk 300 steps—no more, and you'll never visit the medicine store.

—*proverb*

Herbal medicine shops, with their window displays of ginseng roots and attractively packaged medicine bottles are an important part of Chinatown life. Early Chinese immigrants looked to their own culture's well-established traditions to stay healthy in the frontier atmosphere of the mining camps. Herbal remedies eased coughs, treated injuries, and prevented sickness. Today, many Chinatown residents use herbal treatments as well as Western-style medicine. Chinatown's herbalists may have been trained in special medical schools in China, the United States, or elsewhere. And herbal medicine stores are attracting new customers, as knowledge of traditional health ideas becomes more widespread.

The Herb Shop

A unique aroma greets visitors to every Chinatown herb store. Mushrooms, lotus nuts, salted orange peels, strips of bark, and packages of dried fruits fill large bins. Attractive gift boxes of special mushrooms and herbs line the front counter. The glass cases hold acupuncture needles, books, and many types of packaged medicines. You'll also see the traditional filing system used by herbalists—hundreds of small wooden drawers filling an entire wall. Each one holds one kind of root, flower, or stem.

At the polished wooden counter, the herbalist prepares a prescription. Sometimes it is a common remedy requested by a customer. Sometimes it is a mix of 5 to 20 ingredients prescribed by a doctor of traditional Chinese medicine for a patient's special needs. Each item is carefully weighed on a balance scale. Some stems and roots need chopping. Others may need grinding with mortar and pestle. The items are combined, and the mixture is wrapped in paper packets (often one per dose) to be taken home and boiled into a tea.

Herb shops also carry many Chinese medicines that are prepared in modern pharmaceutical factories from traditional formulas. Packaged syrups, pills, and ointments are convenient and popular for colds, aches, and common ailments.

Centuries ago, Daoist hermits living in the mountains of ancient China helped develop the art of herbal medicine. They were seeking the secret for longevity. By trying all kinds of leaves, roots, fruits, and flowers, Daoists learned which plants and foods made them feel healthy and live longer. Over time, this knowledge was studied and shared.

Theories developed, based on the idea of balancing the body's energy. Herbs, like foods, are thought of as having hot or cold characteristics. When taken in the correct doses, herbs can restore the balance of your body. For example, cooling herbs stop a hot fever, warming herbs improve circulation. Each herb (or food) has a special action or way it can change your body, a special nature, and a special flavor (sweet, sour, salty, bitter, or pungent).

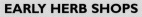

15

Acupuncture

Charts on the traditional doctor's wall or in the herbalist's store show the human body with a pattern of lines. These lines describe pathways called meridians. According to traditional Chinese medicine, a person's energy called *qi* is believed to flow along 12 major meridians.

When you visit the traditional doctor, she checks how well your energy is flowing by taking your pulse—at six different positions on each wrist. Pulses tell about different organs of the body such as heart, lungs, or liver, and inform the doctor if she needs to redirect the body's energy or qi.

Sometimes, traditional doctors use finger pressure (acupressure) or insert very thin needles (acupuncture) on points along the meridian lines to help the qi move. There are over 400 acupoints. Because of how this qi flows through the body, the place pricked may actually be far from the place that needs help. For example, points on the forearms are often used to treat a headache.

Acupuncture has been used in China for about 1,900 years to treat conditions such as arthritis, headache, asthma, and chronic pain. Now it is also used in ways ancient doctors never knew of. It can provide anesthesia for some operations, and can relieve side effects of cancer treatments.

In China today practitioners of Chinese medicine may work along with doctors specializing in Western medicine. Traditional Chinese medicine is becoming an accepted form of health care in the United States. Its practitioners must receive special training, pass exams, and be licensed by their states. They work from their own clinics or offices, or in traditional pharmacies.

Eye Exercises *(Yan Baojian Cao)*

Here is an exercise to relax your eyes when reading or studying. Based on acupoints, it was developed to help China's school children.

Use index fingers to massage lightly and slowly around the eyes working outward along the eyebrows then circling underneath the eyes toward the center.

Hot Chicken *Bu* Soup

On the first day of winter, many families brew hot chicken bu *soup. Bu recipes (meaning food that soothes and makes you feel better) give strength for the cold days ahead. Key ingredients include herbs such as ginger and red dates.*

Bu (po) means to patch up and repair. When talking about medicine and the body, bu *combined with other Chinese words means "to mend" and "to help."*

1 chicken, about 2½ pounds, cut into pieces, skin removed if desired

2 quarts chicken broth

6 dried black mushrooms (shitake)*

2 slices fresh ginger*

6 Chinese red dates (jujubes)*

1 tablespoon green onion, minced

salt to taste

Soak mushrooms in warm water for 10 minutes. Squeeze out water, remove and throw away stems, and cut caps into thirds.

Place chicken and broth in large pot, not aluminum. Add mushrooms, ginger, and dates. Cover and bring to a near boil, lower heat immediately, and simmer for an hour. Top with green onion. Salt to taste.

* You can buy red dates, ginger, and dried mushrooms at food shops or herbal stores. According to herbalists, red dates help your circulation. Ginger, fresh or dried, gets rid of chest colds and stomach aches.

Shouxing: God of Long Life

He's a popular symbol on New Year cards, birthday scrolls, and packages of teas and herbs. You'll recognize him by his long white beard and huge balding head. He carries a peach in one hand and a staff with a magic gourd in the other. He rides a deer or flies on a crane with his embroidered "long life" robes fluttering in the wind.

恭賀新禧
HAPPY NEW YEAR

造燭求明，讀書求理
Zaozhu qiuming, dushu qiuli.
Make a candle to bring brightness, read a book to achieve learning.

—*proverb*

Newspaper racks display Chinese-language papers and magazines. Chinese characters formed from glowing neon tubes announce shops and restaurants. Street signs, posters, and overhead banners spread information in both Chinese and English.

Many Chinatown residents can read and write the Chinese language. Some learned before moving to North America. Others have learned in "Saturday school" or after-school Chinese schools. Children today may be from the third generation in their family to attend these schools. In the 19th century, Chinese organizations and Christian churches began schools for the often-illiterate immigrants, hoping their students would eventually help to modernize China. Today many families think learning Chinese will be useful for doing business with Asia and for maintaining family culture and traditions.

The Stationery Store

At the stationery store, pointed ink brushes arranged by size fill the display cases. There are boxed inkstones and inksticks in every price range. Rolls of writing paper are stacked like logs, one on top of the other.

Here, it's easy to find what you need for practicing calligraphy—"beautiful writing" or *shufa*. Chinese calligraphy is an art form in its own right with rules to follow and tools to master. You start with a carefully selected brush dipped in ink. You must follow an exact order, forming the character's strokes from top to bottom and left to right. The character must fit inside an imaginary perfect square.

Learning calligraphy takes discipline. First you must learn to hold the brush correctly and to make bold, loose brushstrokes. You can spend many hours practicing a single character. Then you might work on an entire poem. Beginners use newspaper. They work to master the brush, to make strokes with beauty and energy, and to create a composition that pleases the eye.

In old China scholars often combined calligraphy with painting and poetry (the three sister arts). Sometimes the artist created both the poem and the painting. Other times he added a poem to another scholar's painting. The style of writing, the heaviness of the ink, and the thickness of each stroke added to the beauty of the words and the painting.

Although they still appreciate and enjoy learning calligraphy, today most people write Chinese with pencils and pens. But they follow the same rules for forming characters. And good handwriting remains important. According to Chinese tradition it's one way to judge a person's true nature.

How to Hold a Brush

An ink brush is not held like a pen or pencil. Hold it straight up and down with the thumb on the one side of the brush and first and second fingers on the other. Keep the wrist stiff and raised comfortably above the paper. Your palm should make a pocket, almost big enough to hold an egg. If you can move the brush with a penny resting on the top, you're holding it correctly.

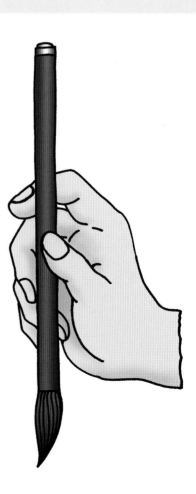

19

Spoken Chinese

In China today the national language is based on the dialect of the North, and known as *tongyongyu* (*putonghua,* Mandarin). It is taught in schools, and used on radio and TV, and over 70% of China's people can now speak it. But in many parts of the country, people speak regional dialects. In the United States, the most well known is Cantonese *(Yue)* the spoken language of the far south (including Hong Kong). Cantonese is as different from Mandarin as French is from Spanish. Even Cantonese has local subdialects, like *Toishan,* named after the region in China, spoken by many older Chinatown residents. In Chinatown you may also hear Hakka *(Kejia),* Fujianese *(Min),* and Shanghainese *(Wu).*

Spoken Mandarin has only about 400 single syllables (English has thousands). Often Chinese words with different meanings can have the same sound like "to," "two," and "too" in English. To help the listener tell words apart, spoken Chinese uses tones. For example, the words for mother, hemp, scold, and horse are all "ma." The difference is that they are spoken with different tones. Mandarin has four.

- a high first tone, —
- a rising second tone, ╱
- a dipping third tone, ╲╱
- or a short fourth tone. ╲

To get an idea of tones, try saying "Can you come?" Then say "Come!" Most people say the first "come" with a rising tone, the second with a dipping tone. Cantonese uses six or more tones.

Although a single Chinese syllable can often stand on its own as a word, most Chinese words are made up of two syllables. For example, *kanjian,* (look see/to see) means "see." *Zhongtou* (clock/head) means "hour."

All of this can cause considerable confusion and misunderstanding. But it also results in a language rich in puns, word play, and humor.

There are several systems for writing the Chinese language phonetically, using the alphabet (called romanization). When U.S. newspapers print Chinese words, they use a modern system called *pinyin,* which is used in the People's Republic of China. In Chinatown, or in older books you may see other ways of spelling words and names— Peking for Beijing, leechee or lichee for lichi.

Seals

Since ancient times, China's poets, painters, and people doing business have "signed" their names with a personal seal or stamper with the characters of their name. But seals didn't start off as stampers—and ordinary people didn't use them. At first, Chinese officials used the stampers, called *chops* as a sign of office to keep important documents secured. The documents were written on bamboo strips that were tied in bundles. A seal left an imprint on the clay used to cover the cords tying the strips together. Unbroken seals showed that nobody had tampered with the document.

Later, paper and silk replaced bamboo strips, and seals could be inked and stamped directly onto the documents. During the Tang dynasty (618–907), officials and collectors started to stamp calligraphy and paintings to show ownership. Later, painters stamped their own works to show authorship. Today, owning a seal links you with the traditions of these officials, scholars, and painters, and, like your signature, shows who you are.

Stationery stores in Chinatown sell blank seals. The bottom is flat, ready to have a name carved on it. Made of polished bone or stone or jade, seals feel smooth and cool. Carved designs on the tops help make each one unique and beautiful.

To make a seal, the carver writes the Chinese words for your name with brush and ink on a piece of paper about one inch square. He pats the slightly damp paper, face up, on the flat bottom of the seal. The characters are transferred—backwards, like mirror writing—onto the seal. The carver cuts away until the characters stand up (relief) or sit below the surface (intaglio).

Stationary stores also sell tiny ceramic pots of red ink paste (originally made from cinnabar and oil) used for stamping.

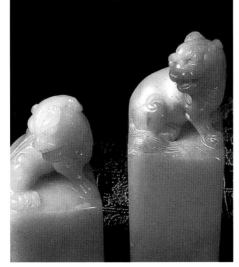

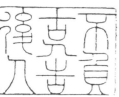

What's in a Character?

Chinese writing uses characters, one for each syllable, instead of an alphabet. Chinese characters tell a story—they're about shape, sound, and meaning. Some Chinese characters are pictographs—signs that in ancient writing look like real things from nature:

日 sun; 人 man; 川 river.

A few describe ideas:

一 one, 二 two, 三 three, 上 above, 下 below.

Still others combine two parts that are complete in themselves to make a character for another word or thought:

木 tree and 木 tree makes 林 forest;

女 woman under a 宀 roof means 安 peace;

女 woman with a 子 child stands for 好 good.

Most characters, however, are made up of parts—a root that tells something about how they sound, and another part, the tag, that gives their meaning. For example, the sound root 風 (*feng*) together with the meaning tag 木 (tree) makes 楓 "*feng*" meaning "maple."

Chinese characters are created from seven basic types of strokes, which must be written in a particular "stroke order." Some characters are simple: 一 *yi* means "one."

Others require many carefully made strokes: 畫 *hua* means "painting."

To write the strokes for a character you usually start from the top left point and end at the lower right point. Other rules are: outside lines before inside, left slanting strokes before right slanting strokes, and for crossing strokes, horizontal before vertical.

The brushstrokes in the character *yong* 永 (eternal) are the basic strokes needed to master Chinese calligraphy:

Writing a character is like building a puzzle. When the parts are finished the whole can be enjoyed—as a picture, a game, a word.

Simplified Characters

Beginning readers need to know at least 2,000 characters to read easy books and newspapers, signs, and menus. They must learn 4,000 to 5,000 characters to be able to read and write college-level Chinese.

To make reading and writing less difficult, China's government adopted an easier way of writing. Since the 1950s simplified characters like 干 for 乾 "dry" and 寿 for 壽 "long life" have been taught in schools and used in newspapers and books. Older Chinatown residents and people from Taiwan still use traditional characters.

Holiday Characters

During the Chinese New Year many people decorate their homes with red banners and scrolls expressing good wishes.

The character (春) *qun* meaning "spring" is often hung upside down (春 like this) because the word for "upside down" in Chinese, *dao,* sounds the same as "to arrive." The meaning becomes "Spring has come!"

"Fortune" and "wealth" written on red paper convey hopes for a happy and fulfilling new year.

一生二，二生三，三生萬物
"Yi sheng er, er sheng san, san sheng wanwu."
"From one comes two, from two comes three, from three the myriads of things."

—*Laozi*, Daode Jing, The Way (Dao) and Its Power

The salesperson at the herb or stationary shop may keep an abacus handy. This ancient calculator, a frame that holds a series of rods with beads on them, has been used in China for over 1,000 years. The first shopkeepers in Chinatown used the abacus to compute everything from costs of rice and grain to weights of gold and silver.

The ancient Chinese thought that numbers maintained order—not only in everyday life, but by helping us understand how we are connected to everything around us. Numbers provided a way of thinking about the universe—the two natural forces of the yin and yang, and the five elements, for example. The abacus kept track of the world here—and beyond.

Today, most Chinatown business people use calculators, cash registers, and computers. The abacus is taught to children to sharpen math skills—and is still used by adults who like its speed.

Abacus

Although it's not clear who invented the abacus or when, the abacus or *suanpan* (calculating tray) was widely used in Chinese households by the 16th and 17th centuries.

Beads on the first rod stand for ones, the second tens, the third hundreds, and so on—like the decimal system. Each bead above the crossbar stands for five of that unit. Each of the beads below the crossbar is worth one unit. The beads are pushed toward the center bar to represent numbers.

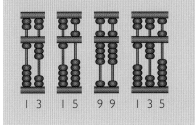

Here is how to represent some numbers:

This is an abacus set at zero.   This is 3,530,757,082.

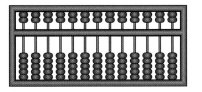

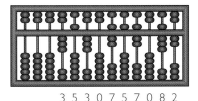

An abacus can be used for addition, subtraction, multiplication, and division. In a math operation when both of the top beads are pushed down, that equals ten. This is carried over by pushing up one bead from the bottom group in the next rod to the left and returning the two top five-beads to the zero position. Using an abacus, it's very easy to write 40,000—you need only one stroke. If you know how to use an abacus, you can add and subtract very quickly.

Counting

At a restaurant, the waiter may tally up the check with familiar Arabic numbers or may use the quick business style, which looks like this:

丨 丨丨 丨丨丨 Ｘ ㄅ 一 二 三 夂 十

The numbers you see in books or on business cards, however, are often written in the regular Chinese style. You can write any number up to 99 in Chinese if you know all of these:

一 二 三 四 五 六 七 八 九 十

For example, 23 is two-tens plus three: 二十三

Combinations of one through ten together with the characters 100 百, 1,000 千, and 10,000 萬 make up the rest.

In China today, Arabic number signs—1, 2, 3, etc.—are used for addresses, clock faces, page numbers, calendars, math and science, measuring, cash registers, and telephone numbers.

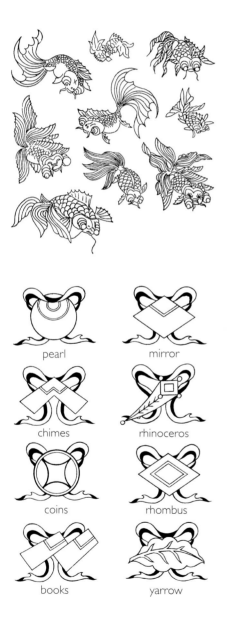

DOUBLE TEN
Each fall many people in San Francisco's Chinatown celebrate Double Ten. Sun Yatsen, the first president of the Republic of China, raised money in American Chinatowns to support the revolutionary movement that toppled the Manchu dynasty on October 10, 1911. His statue stands in St. Mary's Square.

Lucky Numbers

Businesses in Chinatown sometimes use numbers in their name because of the number's special meaning. You may notice a restaurant named *Sihai*, Four Seas. In Chinese, the number four implies many things—the four directions, the four arts (music, chess, literature, and painting), the four seasons. "Four seas" means good food from "everywhere."

Auspicious numbers have been used since ancient times. Today, some people try to get lucky numbers for license plates, phone numbers, and street addresses, and avoid unlucky ones. Here are some more examples of number phrases:

Three Plenties *(Sanduo):* Happiness, many children, and long life. Many food names include the number three, such as Three-Flower Melon Soup. The three Star Gods, Fu, Lu, and Shou, have the power to affect health, wealth, and longevity. They are often seen on New Year's cards.

Fu   Lu   Shou

Five Happinesses *(Wufu):* Long life, good health, riches, honor, and happiness. Five bats stand for the five happinesses because the character for "bat" and "happiness" sound the same, *fu*. Five-spice powder is a common seasoning mix used for roast meats.

Eight Treasures *(Babao):* Pearls, coins, chimes, books, mirror or paintings, rhinoceros horn, a rhombus for good government, and a yarrow leaf. These are the traditional symbols of the scholar. Eight-Treasure Pudding, a dessert, is made from sweet rice (sticky rice) and candied fruits.

Nine Fish *(Jiuyu):* The word for "nine" sounds the same as "to last forever." Banks and stores like to hang paintings with nine fish because they offer the idea of success. Fish sounds the same as "plenty."

Double Happiness *(Shuangxi):* Twice as much happiness. This pair of characters decorates wedding cakes, cards, and presents.

The characters for 100, 1,000, and 10,000 are considered lucky because they mean plentiful, "a great number."

For example, 10,000 *(wan)* means the most of everything, a good luck number— "May 10,000 things happen just the way you wish!" Here are some expressions using 10,000 to mean "all," "everything," or "more than enough":

10,000 corners of the world, *wanfang* = everywhere
10,000 flowers tube, *wanhuatong* = kaleidoscope
10,000 animal park, *wanshengyuan* = zoo
10,000 mile city wall, *wanli changcheng* = the Great Wall

Tangrams

The "seven-piece puzzle," *qiqiaoban*, is said to have originated over 2,000 years ago.

A popular story tells of a tile maker who dropped a square tile on the floor. It broke into seven pieces. As he was trying to put the pieces back into a square he discovered a million other designs were possible too.

These seven simple shapes fit together perfectly in a square. You can move them around to make different designs and pictures, too.

Chinese carpenters played with shapes and forms to make wooden lattice-work for the window openings in palaces, temples, stores, and homes.

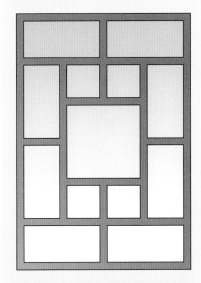

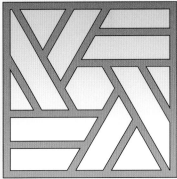

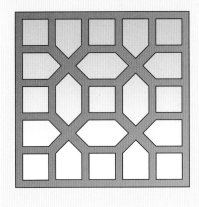

27

Chinese Chess

Chinese chess or *xiangqi* developed during the Tang Dynasty (618–907). It is like a combination of checkers and Western chess. It is probably played by more people than any other board game in the world. Older men play it in the parks, kids play it after school. Stationery stores sell sets. The "board" is a sheet of paper divided into 64 squares. Pieces move from point to point along the lines. A center line (the "river") divides it into two sections. The disk-shaped playing pieces are identified with Chinese characters.

How to Play

The Pieces and Object of the Game Each side controls a 16-piece group made up of a general, two guards, two ministers (or elephants), five foot soldiers, two chariots, two cannons, and two horsemen. The general's palace, which he can never leave, stands out with two diagonal lines. You capture pieces by landing on top of your opponent's pieces. To win is to capture your opponent's general. You also win if your opponent can no longer make a legal move. Pieces move along the lines, from point to point, not from square to square. Players aren't allowed to trap each other into repetitive loops. The trapper has to break it off. Certain pieces have different characters depending on the side of the board they are on. Red goes first. One common opening move is to move your right cannon sideways three points which puts the general "in check." Another is to move the right horseman one forward and one horizontally to the left. Try it!

Moving Pieces

The general, 將 *jiang* or 帥 *shuai,* never leaves the palace. He moves one point at a time in any direction except diagonally. Also, the generals aren't allowed to "see" each other. They can never be directly across from each other unless there is another piece in between.

The guards, 土, 仕 *shi,* flank the general and can only move one point diagonally, backwards or forwards. Also, the guards can't leave the palace.

The ministers or elephants, marked 象, 相 *xiang,* protect the general. They move diagonally two points at a time. The squares moved over must be empty. They cannot cross over the river, either.

The horsemen, 馬 *ma,* or knights start next to the chariots, moving one point forward or sideways to an empty point, then one space diagonally forward. They can't jump over another piece.

The chariots, 車 *che,* begin on the edge farthest away from the general. At each move they can go horizontally or vertically as far as they want. They're also known as cars.

The cannons, 炮 *bao,* start off two ranks in front of the horsemen. They move like chariots except that in order to capture a piece, they have to jump over one other piece. The third piece must lie between the cannon and the enemy. They're also called gun mounts or artillery.

The foot soldiers 卒 *zu* or 兵 *bing,* line up on the fifth rank before the river, with one space between them. While in their own territory they move forward one point at a time. After they cross the river, foot soldiers gain power and can move one space either horizontally or vertically. They can't jump, and can't move backward.

This is how to set up the board:

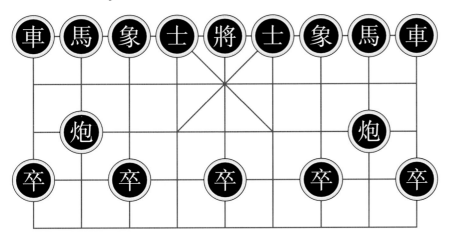

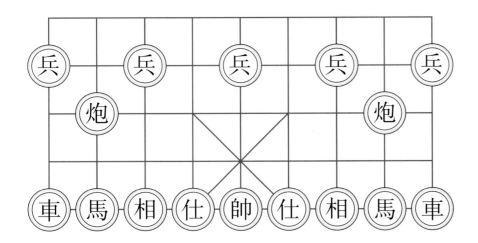

Moves in Chinese chess are written in a special notation. These are two sample moves for opening a game.

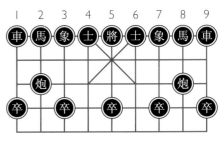

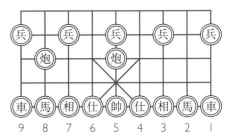

C 2 = 5 (notation)

The white cannon "C" on the second line from the right moves horizontally ("=") to the fifth line from the right. Cannons can move horizontally or vertically as far as they want.

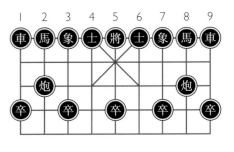

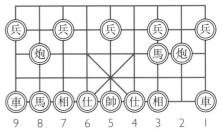

N 2 + 3 (notation)

The white knight ("N") on the second line from the right moves forward ("+") to the third line from the right. Knights move one point in one direction, then one diagonally ahead.

普天同慶
Putian tong qing.
The whole world joins in celebration.

—*saying*

Stilt walkers, floats, high school bands, lion dancers, and pearl-chasing dragons parade through Chinatown. Exploding fire-crackers send up clouds of smoke. Thousands of spectators jam the red-confetti-covered sidewalks. Millions more throughout the United States and Canada are watching the parade on TV. No one wants to leave until the biggest dragon appears. Over 200 feet long, the dragon is carried by a team of 80 dancers. It's San Francisco's biggest public event of the year—the Chinese New Year parade.

Chinatown first celebrated Chinese New Year in 1851. Over time, the celebration grew from a local family event to today's huge festi-val. The parade itself, first held in 1953, is a uniquely Chinese Ameri-can contribution to an ancient calendar cycle.

Dragon Lore

Dragons have been important to China's people since ancient times. In Chinese stories of creation, dragons are helpers and protectors of the gods. Dragons decorate bronze vases made during the Shang dynasty over 3,500 years ago. Beginning with the Han dynasty (206 B.C.E.), dragons came to stand for the power and authority of China's emperors. They represent the spirit of water, and in folk tales are often found in rivers and lakes.

Chinese dragons are benevolent creatures, believed to bring good luck and rain for crops. According to legend, dragons can shrink to the size of a caterpillar or grow large enough to fill the space between the earth and sky. Chinese dragons have a unique shape: the eyes of a rabbit; the head of a camel; the antlers of a deer; the ears of an ox; the body of a snake; the belly of a frog; the scales of a carp; and the claws of an eagle. And when they walk away, they leave the footprints of a tiger.

The Chinese Calendar

When the modern world marked the year 2000, the traditional Chinese calendar was nearing the end of the "year 4697" of the mythical Emperor Huangdi, the "Yellow Emperor." A year has 12, or sometimes 13 months, based on 12 cycles of the moon around the earth. The extra "leap" month is added at certain intervals to keep up with the length of the solar year. Each year begins when the second new moon appears after the winter solstice. The New Year celebration lasts for 15 days until the moon is full again—the Lantern Festival marks this last day. After 12 years are finished, the cycle starts again.

After five 12-year cycles, you've reached one complete cycle of 60 years, the root of the Chinese calendar.

In addition, each year is linked with one of 12 zodiac animal signs: rat, ox, tiger, rabbit, dragon, snake, horse, ram, monkey, rooster, dog, and pig.

31

"Northern" lions are the kind seen in Chinese acrobat performances. They are yellow and red, with long, shaggy hair and manes. Their heads and bodies seem more lion-like. The rear dancer, completely covered by the costume, holds the waist of the head dancer. The dancers must match each other's moves perfectly as the lion skips and prances, plays, rolls, and balances on large balls.

Lion Dancing

First you hear the beat of drums and the blast of firecrackers— RATATATATatatat! Suddenly, a team of lion dancers appears, prancing along the crowded sidewalk. There's a wedding or shop opening to celebrate. Everyone follows. The lion likes to play with the crowd—crouching down and jumping up—shaking its head from side to side. A lion needs two dancers, one for the head and one for the tail. The dancers are usually from martial arts groups or lion dance clubs. The shop owner or wedding couple has invited them. It's hard work. Sometimes the dancers take turns dancing, running out from under their costume while others take their place.

A lion may be accompanied by the Smiling Monk, or Buddha, his master. The monk wears a large pink mask and holds a palm leaf fan. The fan is magical and the monk can tame the lion by waving it. In a routine called "Plucking the Green," the monk takes the lion out to play and look for food.

At the New Year, many "lions" appear, dancing in and out of restaurants and shops. Shopkeepers set out green lettuce for the "lions" to eat. Very skillful "lions" can climb tall poles to eat lettuce leaves placed high up on buildings. (The word for "green" in Chinese sounds like the word for "shared prosperity.") Eating the lettuce and spitting it out sends good fortune. Red envelopes filled with cash are also "fed" to the lion. The money is given to charities and community groups.

How to Do the Lion Dance

It is an honor for martial arts students to be chosen to participate in lion dancing. Lions symbolize everything that is good and protective. For centuries "lions" leaped and turned for emperors and paraded for villagers. Lion dances that mixed acrobatics with special rituals were believed to bring good fortune to the community. Over time the dance grew into a folk dance-drama and a form of New Year entertainment. Today organizations, youth groups, and even police and fire departments sponsor their own lion dance teams.

Most lion dancers are "southern" lions. Their dance style is associated with martial arts that began in southern China. The lead dancer wears a huge, bright, colorful "lion's head" with jaws that snap and large eyes that blink. A long cloth sheet connected to the head stretches over the second dancer. The head dancer controls the lion's eyes and mouth, and raises and lowers the head while dancing. The rear dancer must follow, dancing while stooped over. The heads are made from layers of cloth and papier mâché over a bamboo frame. The biggest lion heads carried by adult dancers may weigh 30 pounds. Lions dance to the beat of a drum, gong, and cymbals.

Want to try it? Beginning lion dancers first learn stances. It is important to know how to lift and move the heavy head.

Next, lion dancers learn to step. The moves should look like a lion's, lively and full of energy. Dancers use walking, trotting, and stances to show the lion's mood. Just like real ones, lions may fall asleep, yawn, look around, stretch, and scratch fleas! Experienced dancers add kicks and leaps, and the best dancers can climb poles, walk balance beams, and stand on each other's shoulders.

HORSE STANCE
Stand strong and square, legs wide apart, with knees slightly bent, like riding a horse. Keep your hands, in fists, at your waist, then raise them straight up and down as you settle into position.

LOW T-STANCE
This move is like an extension of the horse stance. Face forward with both feet parallel as in the horse stance and then lower your body, stretching out one leg to the side while bending the other leg at the knee. Do not bend forward at the waist. Your hands, in fists, begin at your waist, then thrust up and pull inward as you settle into position.

unicorn stance   low t-stance   bow stance   cat stance   horse stance

Festivals

The four most important traditional holidays celebrate the start of a new year, honor the memory of family ancestors, remember the death of an ancient poet, and praise the bright full moon of autumn.

Chinese Lunar New Year (Xinnian)

First day of the first moon—late January or early February

The New Year celebration is the biggest, most important festival. Shoppers visit flower markets to select branches of plum blossoms or quince, and pots of blooming narcissus. Children look forward to receiving their *hongbao* or *laisee,* money-filled small red envelopes, from family and adult friends and neighbors. Homes and shops are decorated with bright posters and hangings with Chinese words for good fortune. Plates of oranges and trays of melon seeds, candies, and dried fruits greet visitors. Throughout the two-week season restaurants are packed with families and clubs holding special holiday dinners. People make plans for the Chinatown parade, scheduled to highlight the Lantern Festival, and greet each other with *Gongxi facai (Gong hay fat choy)*—"Happiness and fortune to all," or *Xinnian kuaile*—"Happy New Year."

Clear and Bright Festival (Qingming Jie)

(April 4th or 5th)

The Clear and Bright Festival honors ancestors and remembers family roots. People visit the graves of their parents and grandparents. They sweep away dirt and cut down weeds. Some families bring fresh oranges and flowers, and arrange pots of sand with sticks of sweet incense for the spirits of the ancestors.

It's kite-flying time, too. Kites in the shapes of centipedes, dragons, and sparrows fly high in the sky of parks and open fields. In China there are international kite competitions.

Dragon Boat Festival (Duanwu Jie)
(5th Day of the 5th Moon)

Brightly painted boats with carved dragon heads at their bows crowd bays and rivers. Twenty people paddle each canoe-shaped boat. A drummer sits in the bow, facing the rowers and setting the pace. Spray flies from thrashing paddles. Faster! The drummers increase the rhythm. Paddlers struggle to stay steady, and keep the pace. One boat pulls ahead, winning the race through muscle power, precise coordination, and the perfect timing of its final sprint.

Dragon boat racing honors Qu Yuan, a poet and patriot of the Chu state during the middle of the Warring States era (475–221 B.C.E.). His advice on how to keep peace with neighboring states was turned down by the emperor. Rejected by the court, he threw himself into the Milo River (in Hunan Province) and drowned. Legend has it that local fishermen searched for him. They beat drums, slapped the water, and fed rice dumplings to hungry fish to prevent them from harming Qu Yuan's body. People from southern China make sticky rice dumplings wrapped in large bamboo leaves for this holiday. Dragon boat racing is now a competitive sport in China, and is catching on internationally. Many cities in the United States now hold annual races.

Moon Festival (Zhongqiu Jie)
(15th Day of the 8th Moon)

The moon festival usually takes place in September, when the full moon is at its brightest. Originally the festival was probably a harvest celebration. Later it became associated with the legend of Chang E. She was exiled to the moon after swallowing the magic potion of long life. If you look closely at the moon, you may be able to see the Jade Rabbit. He keeps Chang E, the Moon Lady, company. Families pack picnic baskets and head for a park, or just sit in their backyard. They gaze at the moon, make wishes, tell stories, sip tea, and snack on oranges and mooncakes—round symbols for the wholeness of family and friends.

RED ENVELOPES

Small red envelopes, *hongbao,* are usually decorated with good-luck slogans and pictures. Grown-ups put money inside (a dollar or two for a young neighbor, more for family) and give them to children at New Year. In the past, copper coins with a hole in the middle were strung together on red twine and called *yasui* money (or *yasuiqian*). In Chinese the word *ya* means "crush" and *sui* "year." The word *sui,* however, sounds the same as "evil." So *yasui* sends the message to do away with evil for the New Year. Red envelopes for money became popular with the development and use of paper currency. In Cantonese, red envelopes are called *laisee,* meaning "profit." Today the terms *hongbao, laisee,* and the traditional *yasuiqian* are all used. No matter what the name, however, the result is the same—a lucky child winds up with quite a bit of spending money. Chinatown banks make sure to have a large supply of crisp new bills on hand.

樹高千丈葉落歸根
Shu gao qianzhang, ye luo gui gen.
A tree may grow 10,000 feet, but
its leaves will return to its roots.

—*proverb*

On New Year's Eve in Chinatown, most families are at home, talking and eating together. It's important to be "around the stove," *weilu*, on the last evening of the year. Some families set out chopsticks for relatives who can't make it home, and even for well-loved ancestors. But New Year's Eve was not always family time. In Chinatown's early years, most residents were single men. Unable to celebrate with family, they organized New Year banquets with others from the same village. Today Chinatown is filled with families, but the banquet custom continues. Family and district associations still hold dinners and annual meetings during the New Year season. People who have moved away from Chinatown return to feast, visit friends, and wish everyone a happy year ahead.

24 Stories About Honoring Parents

In an antique store, a set of 24 colorful embroidered squares covers the top of a polished rosewood stand. Each square portrays a story about filial piety, *xiao,* which means respect for parents. One tells of a boy who grows up and returns home to make his parents laugh in their old age. He tells funny stories and wears colorful clothes. In another, a son goes into the woods dressed as a deer to get deer milk to cure his sick parents. A third tells about a son who fanned his father's bed in the summer to make it cool and who laid on it in the winter to warm it.

These tales make up a collection of folk fables called *24 Stories of Filial Piety.* Filial piety is one of the most important ideas of the Chinese philosopher Confucius, and it is a basic value of traditional family life. Children are taught to care for their parents, even if it means hard work and sacrifice. From a young age they learn to honor their elders and respect their wishes. In earlier times, a wife would have carefully stitched these scenes on silk to show respect for her husband's family and to pass on lessons of virtue to her own children.

Confucius

Confucius (Kongfuzi) (551–479 B.C.E.), was a teacher and government official. He lived in a time when the empire was especially chaotic and corrupt. He argued that order and good government could exist only when people respected their role in the natural order of things. He described the universe as a hierarchy of relationships—emperor to subject, father to son, older to younger, husband to wife. If everyone observed rituals and customs and treated each other with respect, society would be harmonious. He emphasized education, and self-perfection through the arts. His teachings about family and government were so influential that they have shaped Chinese society for more than 2,000 years.

Family Tree

On Sunday afternoons grandparents, aunts, uncles, and cousins like to visit together and enjoy a family meal. *Ayi*, auntie, and *shushu*, uncle on dad's side, pass out oranges, hot tea, and cookies. *Tangdi,* dad's brother's little boy and *biaomei,* mom's sister's little girl, sit at the children's table. *Popo,* grandmother on father's side, offers candies and sweet treats. Grandmother on mother's side, *waipopo,* helps the children build houses with *mahjong* tiles, and great aunt, *gupo* (on dad's side) reads the grandchildren nursery rhymes until they fall asleep. Relatives are named according to who they are related to and by age. Everyone knows just how they fit in! Because of ancestor veneration, some Chinese trace their ancestry back ten generations or more.

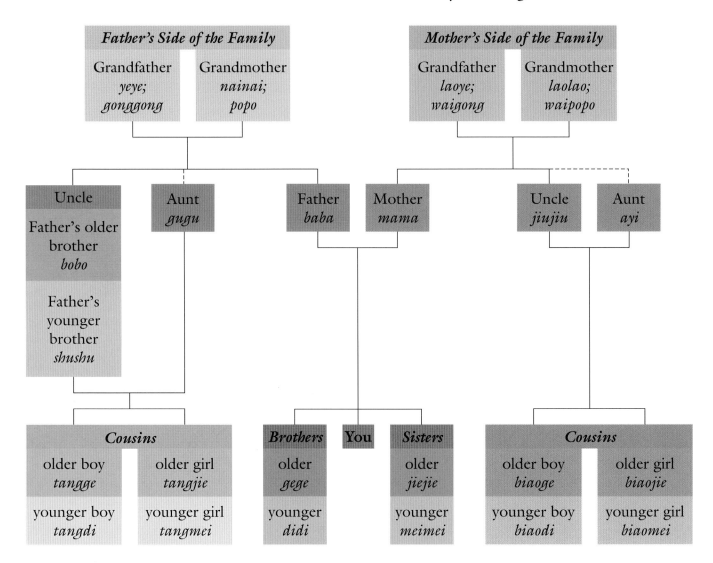

Potstickers

The filling:

½ pound lean ground pork

½ small head of napa cabbage

3 dried black mushrooms, soaked in warm water for 30 minutes

2 green onions, minced

2 cloves garlic, minced

1½ teaspoons fresh ginger, peeled and minced

1 tablespoon soy sauce

1 tablespoon rice wine (optional)

1 tablespoon cornstarch

1 to 2 teaspoons chicken broth

1 teaspoon sesame oil

pinch of white pepper

For wrapping and cooking:

1 pound round potsticker wrappers

4 tablespoons vegetable oil

½ to 1 cup chicken broth

First, mince cabbage (you can use a food processor). Drain off any liquid. You should have 1 to 1½ cups cabbage. Take stems off mushrooms and mince the caps. Mix all ingredients for filling together in a large bowl. Spoon 1 tablespoon of the filling into the center of each wrapper. Fold dough over filling to make a half circle and wet inside edge with a little bit of water. (This helps the two sides stick together.) Pleat edges tightly by making 3 or 4 pleats on the top. Set each potsticker with pleated side up on a baking sheet dusted with flour or cornstarch, so a flat bottom is formed.

To fry: To make potstickers or pan-fried dumplings, *guotie*, heat a large cast iron or non-stick pan. Add 2–4 tablespoons oil. Quickly place potstickers close to one another, around pan, but not touching. Fry until browned on the bottom, 30 seconds to one minute.

Pour in enough broth to cover potstickers half way. Cover the pan and cook over medium heat for 5 or 6 minutes. Uncover, let any liquid cook off, and let brown for 1 to 2 minutes. Use a pancake turner to move them onto a large platter.

Serve with your favorite dipping sauces—chili oil, vinegar, soy sauce, and sesame oil—in small bowls. These dumplings can also be cooked in gently boiling water for 3–5 minutes.

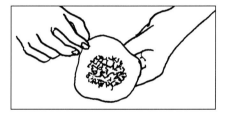

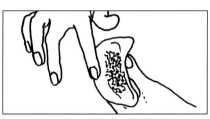

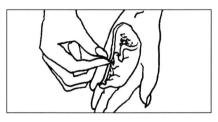

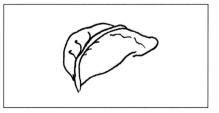

Names

Personal Names

Chinese-American families sometimes give both American and Chinese names, *ming,* to their children. In the Chinese tradition, a good sounding name with a special meaning is believed to bring fortune and success. A name might be something from nature, for example, Mudan (Peony) or Yu (Jade). It might convey a special wish for the child's future: Langshi (Bright Scholar) or Jiale (Happiness).

Some parents still follow the custom of generation names. They give their children names which share a character, as in Hualian and Hualin. *Hua* means "beautiful" or "China"; *lian* mean "lotus" and *lin* means "grove."

The names can rhyme: An*dong* (Peace/East) and An*tong* (Peace/Flowing). In the past, a typical girl's *ming* had to do with virtue or beauty while a boy's *ming* might highlight strong images and attributes such as mountains, dragons, or courage. Nowadays there are no set rules. The choice of names is based on personal preference or family tradition. Names might refer to important events, the seasons, or birthplace.

Family Names

In Chinese, the family name comes first, followed by the personal name (example: Huang Meiling). Your last name or *xing* links you to generations before and those still to come. It is often made up of one character such as Chen or Li. In China today, married women keep their own surnames. Children usually take their father's surname.

Public Names

Older Chinese Americans may be known by more than one name. According to tradition, only close friends and family could call a person by their *ming*. As children grew up, began working, got married, or left their hometown, they often took a new name. This is called a public name or "style" name, *zi*. The characters of this name can sometimes have a meaning related to the original first name. Take, for example, Confucius (Kongfuzi, "Teacher Kong"). His public name was Zhong Ni. His original first name was Qiu. Ni and Qiu commemorate the hill, Ni Qiu, where his parents had prayed for the birth of a son.

Paper Names

Some older Chinese Americans have more than one name because they came to the United States as "paper sons." Laws that kept Chinese from coming to America made some immigrants try desperate measures. Some men paid other Chinese who were already U.S. citzens to sign birth papers claiming them as sons. They could then enter the United States with a new name and identity.

Family Associations

In China there are just over 1,000 common family names for more than one billion people. Chinatown phone books show pages and pages of people with the same family name. But just as all Smiths and Joneses are not blood relatives, neither are all Wangs (Wongs) or Lis (Lees).

The same surnames, however, can link families together. In the past in China, a village or community was sometimes called "the 100 families." Nineteenth-century Chinese immigrants with the same family name formed family associations. Members might not have shared the same uncles and grandparents, but they could often claim descent from the same grand ancestor who lived in ancient times. Family associations helped newcomers find a job and a place to live. Today, family associations host holiday banquets, help new immigrants, provide scholarships, and offer social services.

Families were still a rarity in Chinatown when this photograph was taken in 1904.

殊途同歸
"*Shu tu tong gui*"
"Different paths to attain the
same goal."

—*Yijing, Book of Changes*

An altar shelf over a restaurant's front door, with incense and offerings of fruits; a dragon-pillared temple devoted to Guan Yu, the God of Justice; a European-style church with stained glass and spires; a quiet meditation center—Chinatown offers numerous places to worship. Many Chinese Americans belong to Christian churches, especially those churches whose missions worked with Chinese immigrants in the 19th century. Some are Buddhists or Daoists. Others, especially elders and newcomers observe a blend of beliefs and customs that honors ancestors and a variety of gods. They draw from all of the "three great traditions" of China—Confucianism, Daoism, and Buddhism. For many Chinatown residents, religion is like a garden, a selection of different beliefs and ideas that helps people stay in harmony with the world around them.

Inside the Temple

In San Francisco's Chinatown, a steep stairway leads up to the oldest Chinese temple in the United States. Founded in 1852, it is dedicated to Tianhou, the Goddess of the Sea. A statue of Tianhou, also called Mazu, "grandmother," sits behind the main altar. She wears court robes and the crown of an empress. Large urns hold burning sticks of fragrant incense.

Hanging from the ceiling are red and gold lanterns, each bearing a family name and blessed by the temple. Shelves hold plaques and offerings of oranges. Yellow plaques honor the memory of a deceased relative. Red plaques stand for a living husband or wife. In the center of the room is an altar table; on the front panel are carvings of crabs, fish, and an entire undersea kingdom. People come to temples such as this one to worship many Chinese gods and goddesses. Worshippers place food and small cups of wine and tea on the table to honor Mazu. Others bring stacks of paper "spirit money" to burn as an offering to Guanyin, the Buddhist Goddess of Mercy, or one of the other deities in the temple—the God of Medicine, the God of Learning, the 12 Guardians of Children and Childbirth, or Guan Yu. Worshippers believe the gods and ancestors give help and protection in return for these offerings.

Beliefs

On special days some people also make offerings at home. Joss stores and groceries sell packages of incense and bundles of spirit money to use on important occasions—memorial days, marriages, birthdays. Restaurants and shops often maintain altar boxes, with a statue of Caishen (Choisun), the God of Wealth, or another personal favorite, and offerings of incense and fruit. Souvenir stores sell porcelain statues and posters of gods and of folk heroes. Today, people may not always believe they are directly communicating with the gods, but their offerings are an important symbol of respect. These popular religious beings and folk heroes—along with ancestors—are all part of the different layers of Chinese beliefs. Confucian ideas offer an ordered world—one which honors ancestors, and benevolence, *ren*. Buddhism brings the belief in an afterlife and the hope of nirvana, the end of suffering. And the Daoist religion shows a way to communicate with the invisible world, offering ideas about harmony and balance, nature and change.

A HELPING HAND

In the 1850s, Christian churches, especially Methodist, Congregational, Presbyterian, Baptist, and Catholic began to open missions in China.

As Chinese immigrants began to settle in Chinatown, the church missions followed, providing English classes and social services. Wanting to educate Chinese who would return to help modernize China and to also convince other Chinese to become Christians, the churches established Chinese-language schools as well, for both children and adults. The churches also started the first Chinese-language newspapers in the United States. During decades of anti-Chinese discrimination, these churches were the only non-Chinese groups that consistently supported and helped Chinatown residents. These same churches continue to play an active role in Chinatown today, helping new immigrants, educating children, working for better health care and better housing for Chinatown residents, and assisting the elderly.

Yin and Yang

Expect noise inside a Chinese temple. You may hear the clatter of "moonboards," *bei*, crescent-moon-shaped wooden blocks, dropping to the tiled floor. Rounded on one side and flat on the other, *bei* are used to communicate with the gods. If one lands face down and the other face up, the god's answer is yes; if both flat sides are up, the answer is called double yang and means no; if both flat sides are down, the answer is called double yin and means no.

For temple-goers, yin (cold, shady) and yang (warm, bright) are at the heart of Chinese beliefs. Yin and yang belong together; one cannot be understood without the other. These ideas are part of the teachings of the philosopher Laozi who lived around the same time as Confucius. He taught that people should live in harmony with the cosmic laws that directed the universe. According to Laozi, everything works in cycles, just as day follows night, or season follows season. In later centuries, Laozi's philosophy became the basis for the religion called Daoism. Daoist monks searched for a balanced way of living through diet, breathing techniques, and meditation. They investigated herbs and plants while searching for magic potions that would bring immortality. Magic, spirits, meditation, and various gods aided Daoists in their search for long life and helped take care of everyday problems.

For Daoists, finding out about life's mysteries is about understanding that everything goes around in one direction or another—like yin and yang—and that we are all a part of the cycle of change and fortune. By following the always-changing Dao, The Way, not fighting obstacles but going around them, people achieve enlightenment.

On special days at Chinatown temples, Daoist priests wear richly embroidered robes covered with dragons, cranes, and taiji (yin-yang) symbols.

Buddhism

Chinatowns also support Buddhist centers and temples, where practitioners come to meditate, or to offer flowers and incense to the many representations of Buddha.

Buddha meaning "Enlightened One" was an Indian prince, Siddhartha, who lived during the sixth and fifth centuries B.C.E. He gave up riches and royalty to discover how to overcome suffering and help others. He taught that people can reach an enlightened state called nirvana through meditation and acts of kindness and charity. Followers brought Buddhist ideas to China during the second century C.E. Buddhism became quite popular with emperors and commoners alike. Today millions of people in Asia, as well as in Europe and the United States, practice some form of Buddhism.

Goddess of Mercy

Guanyin, or "one who hears sounds of the world," is honored as a protector of women and children. Sometimes she holds a dove, a necklace of pearls and a vase of balm. Guanyin was once a male Buddhist god, but over the centuries became portrayed as a goddess in robes.

Temple-Building

During the 19th century, immigrants built temples in Chinese communities throughout California. Building and maintaining temples brought people together. They worked hard to find furnishings for the temples, pay for repairs, and set up festival holidays. In California's often rough, unsophisticated rural towns, where anti-Chinese attitudes were strong, temples declared the Chinese presence. While Chinese sojourners to California came and went, the temples stood for permanence, culture, and a Chinese way of life. Non-Chinese called the temples "joss houses" because of the practice of burning joss sticks, or incense, for devotion. Today only a few remain. You can visit the Kong Chow Temple (1853) in San Francisco, Wom Lim Miao (1874) in Weaverville, Bok Kai Miu (1880) in Marysville, and Liet Sheng Kong (1863) in Oroville.

TEMPLE TIES
In old China temples were at the heart of village life. In the temple square, old men read newspapers and played musical instruments under shady trees while children ran over temple steps worn smooth with use. Traveling performers presented operas and puppet shows. At harvest time grain was dried in the wide, open courtyard. In 19th century America, Chinese-owned stores took the place of temple squares. The back of the store was where workers gathered to chat with friends, read a letter from home, play cards, and share an often lonely life.

With land at a premium in Chinatown, temples were often located on the top floors of buildings. In the 1930s, the Kong Chow Temple occupied the third floor and a school the first floor of this building.

龍飛鳳舞
"Longfei fengwu."
The dragon flies and the phoenix dances.

—a saying for a good artist, meaning she paints with "a powerful brush and flowing ink."

Beautiful paintings in the traditional style are everywhere. Delicately brushed watercolors of lotus and chrysanthemums, or cloud-swept mountain crags decorate restaurant walls. Art shops sell careful reproductions of works by famous painters. A street artist shapes lively monkeys from a few bold strokes.

Traditional brush painting, called *guohua,* has been valued in Chinese culture for centuries. Like calligraphy, it requires study and practice. To paint well was one of the signs of a scholar. Even today many people learn brush painting as a hobby. Chinatown shops sell brushes, inks, and paper, and cultural centers offer classes to children and adults.

Inside the Gallery

Salespeople straighten up their shop for weekend buyers. Someone dusts the rosewood benches. Another hangs new scrolls by size on racks. Yet another stacks unframed paintings against the wall and brings out souvenir bookmarks and name cards—Aaron, Bill, Carol—brushed in English and Chinese.

Visitors can see many types of Chinese painting styles here. There may be a flower painting that shows every vein in the leaf. This is called *gongbi hua* (craftsman-brush painting). Other works use loose, suggestive brushstrokes and soot-black ink, with details in deep, full color. These are in the bold *xieyi hua*, "ideas and feelings painting" style, used by Qi Baishi and other 20th century masters.

Visitors will probably notice that most paintings are based on nature. From the 10th to early 18th century, leading Chinese painters focused on landscapes. They painted mountaintops filled with dots, *dian,* and sharp-edged rocks made with axe-cut strokes, *cun.* Song dynasty (960–1279) painters such as Fan Kuan and Guo Xi made you feel the smallness of humanity compared to the immensity of nature. Later, paintings weren't expected to look like anything in nature. Instead, the way a picture was painted told you about the artist. Distant mountains painted in sketchy strokes were the direct expression of feelings. Brushstrokes expressed one's character and feelings just as they had in calligraphy.

Other important subjects are birds, flowers, and animals. Plums, orchids, bamboo, and chrysanthemums became symbols of the ideal gentleman—cultivated, gentle, and strong. Painters represented these flowers in ink-monochrome (black ink on white paper). Black in traditional Chinese painting is itself a powerful kind of color, ranging in value from heavy black to light gray. Some painters use black alone to emphasize the expressive power of brushstrokes. Others add delicate touches of color—mineral blue, crimson red, Indian yellow.

In old China not all painting was done on silk and paper. The gallery also sells copies of images of Buddhist gods painted 1,000 years ago on cave walls in Dunhuang, along the Silk Road. There are reproductions of Han dynasty lacquer cups and Neolithic pottery with painted designs. We don't know who these artists were, but as in more modern paintings, line is everything.

TOURIST CHINATOWN

Many early immigrants were illiterate and had little money for the arts. But as Chinatowns developed, rich merchants wanted better things for a better life. Stores imported beautiful silks, furniture, antiques, paintings, and art supplies.

In the early 20th century, discrimination and the lack of other jobs combined with the interests of San Francisco's Chinatown and city business leaders to create the Chinatown tourist industry. By the late 1930s Chinatown was San Francisco's most popular attraction. Tour bus companies brought visitors by the thousands. Art galleries and souvenir stores flourished. The fortune cookie was invented to please tourists wanting dessert. For the tourists, Chinatown was a foreign place, an exotic spectacle of tiled roofs, unfamiliar arts, unusual foods, and exciting if untrue stories about crime and strange lifestyles. For Chinatown's residents, tourism provided income at a time when jobs were few and Chinese excluded from most, when Chinese children were not allowed to go to school with white children, and when families lived crammed into rooms at the back of shops.

Four Treasures

Many of the same brushstrokes used in calligraphy are also used in painting. Painters use:

- Pointed brushes usually made from natural materials with handles of lightweight bamboo or wood.
- A dry inkstick (made from pine soot mixed with glue) which is rubbed on an inkstone, a stone slab, to make ink. The inkstone has a flat surface for grinding the ink stick into powder and a deep area, or well, to hold water that becomes ink when mixed with the powder. Artists and calligraphers can make the ink thick and heavy or add more water to make it thin and pale.
- Special paper, made from vegetable fibers or the inner white bark of young trees. This type of paper absorbs ink so that many shades of black, gray, or color are possible.

Brushes, inks, inkstones, and paper are called the Four Treasures. They help give Chinese painting its special look and feel. Together with brush pots, seals, and water containers they are appreciated as art objects and collectibles in their own right. Chinatown shops sell the Four Treasures boxed together in special sets.

An Example from a Chinese Artist

For Chinese artists, the brush never seems to rest. In this picture, Wang Hui, a Qing dynasty painter (1644–1911), tries to balance form and space—as a rule a Chinese painting is about one-third form and two-thirds space.

Brush Painting—Step by Step

Painting in the Chinese style requires learning how to use different brush strokes.

Try it! Practice these examples from the *Painting Manual of the Mustard Seed Garden*. Put them together to create your own landscape. Try doing the same scene for different seasons—using bare trees and snow for winter and full foliage for summer.

Follow these step-by-step methods for painting a bird:

(1–4) Start with the beak. Make a hook stroke and place the eye above the beak. Fill in the top of the head, and brush in feathers around the neck and shoulders.

(5–7) Make circular brushstrokes (small and large) and tapering strokes (long and short) for the body— draw in the wing tips and carefully brush in the tail.

(8–9) The breast of the bird is in front of the legs. Save the legs for last. With a quick stroke, draw the feet curled as if to grasp the branch of a tree or spread out for standing lightly on the ground.

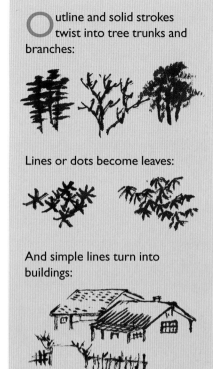

Outline and solid strokes twist into tree trunks and branches:

Lines or dots become leaves:

And simple lines turn into buildings:

| 1–4 | 5–7 | 8–9 |

49

lotus—pure, sweet, and in harmony

Picture Symbols

In the antique store, huge pots and vases may be decorated with flying bats, *fu,* for good luck and deer, *lu,* for long life. A set of dishes has pink peaches of immortality around the rim. Animals, little birds, and blossoming flowers can mean happy wishes, good fortune, and success. These designs were often used on bowls and vases, especially during the Ming (1368–1644) and Qing (1644–1911) dynasties. It was thought that if you surrounded yourself with lucky images your dreams might come true.

Some things represent ideas. A gold brick means riches; a pomegranate fruit, because of its many seeds, stands for families filled with children. Sometimes, the symbol plays on words with the same sound. For example, the bat, whose name is *fu,* sounds like the word for "fortune" or "blessings." These visual puns or rebuses are very popular in Chinese art.

Hidden messages that were understood centuries ago are still found everywhere in Chinatown—in restaurants, card shops, clothing stores, and markets. You can find these motifs as jewelry designs, as papercuts, as computer clip art. Symbols of harmony and good fortune are the most popular.

narcissus—fresh beginnings

Symbols

Here are some favorite symbols, for gifts, for names:

white cranes, pine—long life

red bats and coins—blessings in front of your eyes (because "gold coins" and "in front of your eyes" sound alike)

pine, bamboo, and plum—three friends of winter (loyalty, nobility, and truthfulness)

butterflies—birthday greetings, ("butterfly" shares the same sound as the word for "octogenarian"

dragon and phoenix—peace and good tidings for weddings (the dragon is the symbol of the king, the phoenix of the queen; placed together they are symbols of honor, riches, and good fortune)

carp jumping over a dragon door—achievement, good career (in legend, carps that jump over the Dragon Gate become dragons)

50

The Eight Immortals

These popular Daoist figures are often used as wedding and birthday decorations. Legend has it that they brought birthday gifts to the God of Long Life. There are many stories about them and about how they achieved immortality. You'll find them portrayed on wedding and birthday cards, on carvings in restaurants, on kites and lanterns.

Here is how to identify them:

Zhongli Quan, the leader, carries a magic fan.

Zhang Guolao rides a white mule (backwards!) that he can shrink and tuck in his wallet when not in use. He carries a drum and drumsticks.

Lü Dongbin wears a sword on his back for slaying monsters, and carries a magic fly-whisk. He tells riddles and is a friend to all who need a friend, especially children.

Cao Guojiu is a court official. He carries a pair of clackers.

Li Tieguai, a master of daydreaming, once left his body for several days. When he returned his body was gone. The only replacement he could find was that of a beggar. He carries a crutch to help him walk and a gourd filled with magic herbs for healing people.

Han Xiangzi is a mischief-making poet who plays the flute. He is the patron of musicians.

Lan Caihe is a young women who likes to sing. She carries a lute or flower basket. In some stories this is a young man, the patron of gardeners, a beggar who sang for his living.

He Xiangu walks long distances gathering herbs and fruits. She holds a lotus flower or seed pod.

Cao Guojiu

Zhongli Quan

Lü Dongbin

Lan Caihe

Li Tieguai

He Xiangu

Han Xiangzi

Zhang Guolao

各有所長
Ge you suo chang.
Each person possesses a special talent.

—*saying*

In the community center, girls and boys are working on martial arts routines. Others learn to flutter long winding ribbons used in a folk dance. Nearby, musicians tune their instruments—a two-stringed *erhu*, a moon-shaped *yueqin*. Another group hurries to ready their float for the New Year's parade.

In the 19th century, traveling performers were Chinese villagers' main source of culture and entertainment. Storytellers, puppeteers, and opera performers acted out stories and folktales. Even illiterate villagers knew of the adventures of the Monkey King, a character in a novel. Today, Chinatown's cultural centers may schedule a face painter from Beijing or a puppet troupe from Shanghai. Their workshops, classes, and lessons help kids keep alive the traditions of their parents and experiment with new techniques in art, music, and dance.

Once Upon a Time . . .

Along with politicians and notables, Miss Chinatown and her court, costumed children and martial arts students, the Chinese New Year's Parade usually includes a cast of characters from favorite Chinese stories. Elaborate floats and marchers with big papier mâché masks and embroidered silk costumes always bring cheers from the crowd. People point to their favorites:

Monkey King, the rebellious hero in the novel *Journey to the West* (written by Wu Cheng'en over 500 years ago), who can somersault more than 100,000 miles and turn his breath into a mighty wind. Holding his magic staff and wearing a tiger skirt, Monkey protects the monk, Tripitaka (Xuanzang), who you can recognize by his golden crown and long, flowing robes. Their two friends Pigsy and Sandy accompany them on their journey to find sacred Buddhist scriptures. Performers acting the role of Monkey flip, leap, and roll.

Hua Mulan, who took the place of her aging father as a soldier. No one knew she was a girl until she returned home after 14 years, and with awards from the emperor. Today children in Chinese school still learn the sixth-century poem, "The Song of Mulan."

Guan Yu with his red face (for bravery), sword, and armor. He comes from a time when no one knew whether China could ever be whole again. In the historical novel, *Romance of the Three Kingdoms,* written six centuries ago by Lo Guanzhong, Guan Yu, along with his two friends Zhang Fei and Liu Bei, tries to bring back the fallen Han dynasty. Because of his loyalty and bravery, people honor him as a god of justice.

Other favorite parade characters include fierce outlaws with names like **Black Whirlwind** and **Tiger Killer** from the popular 14th century novel *Outlaws of the Marsh (Water Margin).* Many are heroes who, having suffered at the hands of corrupt officials, help the poor by challenging the rich with skillful martial arts and a virtuous code of honor.

Always admired are the elegantly dressed young women riding a float that looks like the mansion in *Dream of the Red Chamber.* This still-popular, many-charactered, 200-year old novel examines a rich family's dreams and vanities, and a tragic love affair.

These stars of legend and history are an active part of today's Chinese culture. Grandparents know their stories and pass them on to their grandchildren. Girls and boys read about them in comics, watch them in movies, in cartoons and dramas on TV, or in Chinese opera shows at the theater.

The first Chinese opera in the United States opened to a packed crowd in San Francisco in 1852. By 1880 there were eight theaters. Today there are none. Chinese-language radio and TV often broadcast traditional operas and cultural centers sponsor live performances.

Chinese Theater

In a crowded theater, the house lights dim. The stage is bare, except for a table. A cymbal begins a rhythmic clamor. Suddenly, a fierce general wearing huge shoes, a tall headdress, and a bright, embroidered costume with padded shoulders saunters onto the stage. The flags rising from his back (which show he is a general) flutter with every move he makes.

As the general begins to sing, his arm and hand gestures reveal what's happening. He shows that he's angry by stepping back and flinging his overlong sleeves forward. If he waves a tasseled stick, he is riding a horse. If he presses his hands together, he's slamming a door. The beat of the cymbal and of a wooden clacker gives more clues, faster and louder for the exciting moments, with changing rhythms that follow the movements of a soldier's sword fight or a leading lady's distress.

This is Chinese opera. It includes music, dance, mime, acrobats, and drama. Chinese audiences have enjoyed opera for over 800 years. Authors and composers are often unknown. Music and stories are based on folk melodies and tales. There's neither scenery nor sets. Although many Chinatown residents prefer other regional styles, the best known today is Beijing opera. Traveling troupes from China have introduced modern audiences to this distinct art. Beijing opera, from the north, is flashy and fast-paced, with energetic, bright singing, and heavy use of percussion instruments. It is very stylized. Elaborate make-up and costumes mark different characters. Yellow dragon gowns for emperors; bright silk robes for gallant young heroes; colorful face-painting for daring warriors. Actors show their intentions partly by the expressions on the face, but also through stylized movements, like mimes. The audience knows how to interpret the movements, costumes, and face paint. It can be exciting, with lots of acrobatics, clowning, and martial arts.

Chinese American opera productions feature more dramatic staging. Dragons rise up out of the earth. Gods come down from the heavens. A 20-piece orchestra of Chinese and European instruments may play in a non-traditional way. Such changes are to be expected. It's part of the bridge between then and now, East and West.

Monkey King and his magic staff in a performance by a visiting Beijing opera troupe from China.

Every Face Tells a Story

Actors playing warriors, bandits, and heroes in Chinese opera paint their faces with bright colors and bold patterns to define their character for the audience. These are *jing,* or painted-face characters. A red face shows goodness and strength; a white face stands for evil and cunning. A face painted with a few strokes stands for someone honest and true. Patterns with many lines show someone who is untrustworthy or evil. Souvenir stores often carry miniature clay masks showing face-painting styles, *lianpu.* You can tell good from bad if you remember these basic rules:

	Color
Heroes	red: loyal and brave
	black: honest and forceful
	purple: quiet and strong
Villains	white: sly and cruel
	yellow: cunning and brutal
Warriors and Bandits	blue: fierce and bold
	green: stubborn and violent
Supernatural Spirits	gold: Buddhist gods
	silver: powerful spirits

Jing characters in Chinese opera wear face make up in specific patterns. Female roles use white and pink make-up to highlight rosy cheeks and pale skin.

Martial Arts

On Saturday afternoons, kids and grownups pack Chinatown's movie theaters. The most popular movies are martial arts films. Most are made in Hong Kong and the language is Cantonese. The themes and plots have their roots in China's traditional stories. On the screen, heroes and enemies jump into the sky and fight off ghosts and demons. Some heroes are ordinary people, some have special powers. They practice martial arts to protect people and keep their honor.

The Chinese term for martial arts is *wushu*. Movies and TV show some of the many different fighting styles based on fast punches, strikes, kicks, and blocks. The Iron Lohan, for example, requires forearms as tough and hard as iron for skillful blocking. The Crane master, thin with arms like stalks, uses striking postures to win a fight. The Monkey master, always moving, walking and jumping, does dozens of flips and kicks.

Actors might also learn special theatrical martial arts styles. They might use double-edged swords in some routines and spears and halberds in others, sparring and thrusting, jumping and somersaulting. Teachers instruct them not to mix styles because each routine has its own personality.

In Chinatown, people learn martial arts for sport and relaxation. Martial arts provide a way of learning discipline, behaving, breathing, and concentrating. Developing internal energy is as important as building external strength and muscle. Students learn to train so that mind and body become one.

Students from martial arts schools demonstrate their school's forms and styles in parades and for community events. The best students also perform the lion dance for martial arts contests and neighborhood celebrations.

Many of the styles grew from exercises taught by Bodhidharma, a sixth-century Indian monk who traveled to China, and is known as the founder of Zen Buddhism.

Popular styles in U.S. Chinatown schools include *Choy Li Fut, Hung Gar,* Southern and Northern Shaolin, and *Wing Chun.*

56

The Music Store

A row of shiny metal gongs, *luo,* hangs from a stand in a music store near a large double-faced drum. A visitor tries out a flashy pair of cymbals, *bo,* and sends out a thunderous clash. Traditional Chinese percussion instruments such as these are used for lion dances and opera performances. Musicians play *luogu yue,* gong-and-drum music, for festivals and processions. The loudest rhythm comes from the thundering "big drum," *dagu.* The top face of the drum is higher in pitch than the bottom. Another rhythm keeper is the hand clapper, *ban,* made from two hardwood sticks. It is held in one hand and swung from side to side, like castanets.

Cymbals, drums, and gongs mark the steps for lion dancing and the movements of characters in opera. The edges of a pair of round metal cymbals can be clashed together to make a sharp, crisp sound, or brushed for a softer, swishing sound. A gong can follow the moves of a lion or announce the entrance of the leading lady. It is struck with a covered mallet to make a variety of sounds that vibrate in the air long after the first strike.

The music store also sells traditional string and wind instruments. Hanging on the wall are *pipa* (a pear-shaped lute) and *yueqin* (a round four-stringed "moon guitar"). Stands hold *zheng* (a bridged zither with at least 16 strings) and *qin* (a long seven-string zither without frets), both played by plucking. There are bowed-string instruments, like the two-stringed *erhu* and smaller *jinghu.* And there is the *yangqin,* a box-shaped dulcimer played by striking its strings with bamboo sticks.

Wind instruments include *dizi* (horizontal bamboo flutes) and *suona* (oboe-type instruments with double reeds and a large copper bell like a trumpet.) The *sheng* is a bundle of 17 bamboo tubes inserted into a bowl, played by blowing a spout-like mouthpiece.

An orchestra accompanying Chinese opera might include *erhu* and *jinghu, dizi, sheng,* and *yueqin* along with drums, clackers and cymbals. *Pipa, zheng, sheng, dizi,* and *erhu* are used in orchestras and as solo instruments. *Qin,* an ancient instrument long associated with scholars and royalty, is a solo instrument. *Suona* is used in folk music, dances, and processions, often joining drums and gongs.

Many Chinese musical instruments, including the *pipa, sona,* and *yangqin,* originated in Central Asia and the Middle East.

bo

erhu

suona

sheng

dagu

luo

57

Families, groups of teenagers, and elderly couples stand shoulder-to-shoulder at the dimsum house. Everyone is chatting. Almost as much Mandarin as Cantonese is being spoken. People are discussing family, sports, jobs, movie stars. Someone points out the new mall that replaced the old theater down the street. Someone else mentions their uncle's new bakery, way out on Mission Street. One family is celebrating a daughter's college admission. Another plans the grocery shopping to be done before driving home to the suburbs.

Chinatown keeps changing. Many older residents and their children have moved to the suburbs or other neighborhoods. The civil rights movement of the 1960s overturned discriminatory laws and opened up job, education, and housing opportunities for Chinese Americans. There are more choices. The younger generations move on. The Chinese American story is much bigger than the story of Chinatown.

Storefronts now host new businesses, where newcomers, often from Hong Kong, South China, or Vietnam are as determined to succeed as were earlier immigrants. And Chinatown shops also sell electronics, backpacks, soap, and other modern products that today's China offers the world. The old Chinatowns have expanded beyond their traditional boundaries. They're as crowded as ever. Thousands of people emigrate to the United States each year from China and other Asian countries. Many immigrants still start out their new life in the oldest Chinatowns—San Francisco, New York, Los Angeles, Boston, Chicago, Oakland, Vancouver. Today, 60% of the residents of San Francisco and New York Chinatowns are newcomers. As in previous eras, many are young men hoping to find their own Gold Mountain. They often bring little but an adventurous spirit, and a willingness to work hard. Other immigrants arrive with their families, or join family already here. Chinatown's newest residents include highly skilled professionals, factory workers, elderly people, and babies. Life in the old Chinatowns can be a challenge. Housing is in short supply, especially for families and the elderly. Restaurant and sewing jobs don't pay much. Too many people work long hours for low pay. Caught between old and new, some young people come adrift. But as in the past, Chinatowns offer newcomers a lively community, a familiar language and culture, jobs, the support of youth centers, community organizations, social services, churches, senior care, and a sense of continuity.

Communities shaped by racism and discriminatory laws, fueled by pride and a long history of solidarity and community, graced by rich cultural traditions, Chinatowns are unique.

Come and visit. Walk in the footprints of the people who live here, look through the eyes of those who call this place home, learn, enjoy, have fun!

Old and new, roots and branches. The Chinatown story continues.

When the future looks back
It is like the present looking at the past:
Things pass by but they are never gone.

—*couplet, anonymous*

逝者如斯未嘗往
後之視昔亦猶今

59

Other Chinatowns in the United States

Oakland, California

Oakland's Chinatown rose and fell several times following the Gold Rush years. In the 1870s, it came into its own as Chinese railroad workers, farmers, and fishermen lost jobs and sought work in cities. San Francisco Chinese sought refuge across the Bay after the 1906 earthquake and fire, and some stayed on to make their homes there. World War II fueled a boom that helped many Chinatown families achieve financial security. Today, this lively, growing Chinatown serves downtown "Oaktown" workers as well as everyday needs of a resident community with roots in China, Vietnam, Laos, the Philippines, and Cambodia. Huge crowds turn out for its annual street fair, and its Lunar New Year celebration is a Pan-Asian event.

New York

Largest in the United States, and home to the majority of New York's Chinese population, this densely populated community began in the 1870s, when Chinese left the West looking for new opportunities. With an estimated 250,000 residents, and occupying six times its original area, Chinatown's population has quadrupled since the 1960s, spreading into Manhattan neighborhoods originally settled by earlier waves of Italian, Irish, and German immigrants. Today thousands of newcomers work in Chinatown's restaurants, garment factories, and jewelry trade. New York also has "new" Chinatowns, in Queens and Brooklyn.

Los Angeles

Los Angeles has two Chinese communities. New Chinatown began as a Chinese American development after the original Los Angeles Chinatown was demolished in the 1930s to make way for a railroad terminal. A central plaza with artist-designed gates and a pagoda anchor a community of 14,000. In recent years Monterey Park, a suburb, has become home to many people originally from Hong Kong and Taiwan.

Chicago

When the Transcontinental Railroad was completed in 1869, many out-of-work Chinese headed for Chicago. Although its population doubled to 14,000 in the 1960s, urban development and expressway building split the community and pushed it south, with no room to grow. Still, like other Chinatowns, it continues to provide homes and jobs for new immigrants and elders. Newcomers, especially Chinese from Vietnam, have found more space along "Argyle Street," on the north side.

Boston

Another community with roots in the 1870s, Chinatown is home to about 5,000 residents, a 300% increase over the last decade. It provides many who immigrate from Asia to New England with their first address, with social services, cultural activities, and support organizations. But the building of expressways and the expansion of public institutions have cut into its borders, and land and housing are in short supply.

Philadelphia

Small, compared to others, its compact neighborhood has many of the same features as other Chinatowns—restaurants, markets, gift shops. A montage of architectural decorations, including carved dragons, ornamental gates, and pagoda-style roofs, create a colorful atmosphere.

Honolulu

Beginning in the 1850s, Chinese were recruited to work on American-owned sugar and pineapple plantations in the Hawaiian Islands. After completing their work contracts, many opened stores and other businesses, especially in downtown Honolulu (around River Street). As immigration was not controlled by U.S. laws until 1898, Chinatown was always a family community. It was destroyed and 4,000 people left homeless in 1899 when the fires set to burn homes of bubonic plague victims got out of control. Finally rebuilt, the community did well in the 1930s, as the tourist cruise industry discovered Hawaii. Today's Chinatown is a well-established mix of Asian and Hawaiian culture, with art stores, noodle factories, and lei shops. Like other Chinatowns it copes with meeting needs of new residents while facing pressure from urban development.

Other cities with historic Chinatowns include Seattle and Washington, D.C. Houston, whose Asian population grew from 14,000 in 1980 to 200,000 in 1995 has both an older downtown Chinatown and a large new community.

Chinatowns in Canada

Vancouver

Some Chinese went north during the California Gold Rush and more followed later to work in western Canada's mills, mines and fisheries. The 1880s brought over 10,000 more to build the Canadian Pacific Railway. Chinese in Canada also faced discriminatory laws and racism. Many retreated to Vancouver, then a small, frontier town. In 1927 Canada halted immigration from China and the community remained small. But in the 1960s it was able to block a redevelopment project that threatened its residential area. Recent changes in Canadian laws encouraged new immigrants, especially from Hong Kong, who have helped finance new development. Now, 30% of Vancouver's residents are of Chinese descent, and Chinatown is a lively, rapidly growing center for both residents and tourists.

Toronto

Beginning in the 1970s, changes in Canada's immigration laws attracted many new immigrants to Toronto. Over 100,000 Chinese live in Toronto's main downtown Chinatown. It serves tourists and residents with restaurants, antique stores, markets, bakeries, and herb shops. Its Kensington Market is a multiethnic showplace reflecting Toronto's diverse population. There are now four other Chinatowns in the Toronto area, as well.

BIBLIOGRAPHY

San Francisco's Chinatown

Fong-Torres, Shirley. *San Francisco Chinatown: A Walking Tour.* Berkeley: Pacific View Press, 2001.

Genthe, Arnold, and John Kuo Wei Tchen. *Genthe's Photographs of San Francisco's Old Chinatown.* New York: Dover Publications, 1984.

Hoobler, Dorothy. *The Chinese American Family Album.* New York: Oxford University Press, 1994.

Lai, Him Mark, Genny Lim, and Judy Yung. *Island: Poetry and History of Chinese Immigrants on Angel Island, 1910-1940.* Seattle: University of Washington Press, 1996.

McCunn, Ruthanne Lum. *Thousand Pieces of Gold.* San Francisco: Design Enterprises of San Francisco, 1981.

Wong, Jade Snow. *Fifth Chinese Daughter.* New York: Harper, 1950.

Yep, Laurence. *The Case of the Goblin Pearls.* New York: HarperCollins, 1997.

————. *Lion Dance.* New York: HarperCollins, 1998.

————. *Firecrackers.* New York: HarperCollins, 1999.

Yung, Judy. *Chinese Women of America: A Pictorial History.* Seattle: University of Washington Press, 1993.

Chinese Culture for Children

Aria, Barbara. *The Spirit of the Chinese Character.* San Francisco: Chronicle Books, 1992.

Demi. *The Dragon's Tale.* New York: Henry Holt, 1996.

————. *Happy New Year.* New York: Crown Publishers, 1997.

Goldstein, Peggy. *Long is a Dragon.* Berkeley: Pacific View Press, 1992.

Kraus, Robert and Debby Chen/Wenhai Ma (illus.). *The Making of Monkey King.* Union City, California: Pan Asian Publications, 1998.

Lee, Huy Voun. *At the Beach.* New York: Henry Holt, 1994.

————. *In the Snow.* New York: Henry Holt, 1995.

————. *At the Park.* New York: Henry Holt, 1998.

Lee, Jeanne M. *The Song of Mulan.* Arden, North Carolina: Front Street, 1995.

Levine, Steven I. *The China Box.* Boulder: Boulder Run Enterprises, 1998.

Mitchell, David. *The Young Martial Arts Enthusiast.* New York: Dorling Kindersley, 1997.

Shen Krach, Maywan/Hongbin Zhang (illus.). *D is for Doufu.* Auburn, California: Shen's Books, 1997.

Shen Krach, Maywan, and Maychi Shen Wang/Youshan Tang (illus.). *I Love China.* Auburn, California: Shen's Books, 2000.

Stepanchuk, Carol. *Red Eggs & Dragon Boats.* Berkeley: Pacific View Press, 1994.

Tan, Amy, and Gretchen Shields (illus.). *The Moon Lady.* New York: Maxwell Macmillan International, 1992.

Tempert, Ann, and Robert Andrew Parker (illus.). *Grandfather Tang's Story.* New York: Crown Publishers, 1990.

Williams, Suzanne/Andrea Fong (illus.). *Made In China.* Berkeley: Pacific View Press, 1996.

Young, Ed. *Monkey King.* New York: HarperCollins, 2001.

Yep, Laurence/Kam Mak (illus.). *The Dragon Prince.* New York: HarperCollins, 1997.

Zheng Zhensun and Alice Low. *A Young Painter: The Life and Paintings of Wang Yani.* New York: Scholastic, 1991.

Note: We have used the pinyin romanization system to write Chinese words. This is the official system adopted by the People's Republic of China for standard Chinese and the romanization most often used by U.S. newspapers and magazines. Commonly used Cantonese words are occasionally included following the pinyin. There is no one standard Cantonese romanization. Our spelling may differ from other versions in books and newspapers or on signs and menus.

The pinyin, "c" is pronounced like ts, as in bats, "zh" is like j, as in jump, "q" is like ch, as in chew, and "x" is like sh, as in shoe.